Christ-centred Renewal

Christ-centred Renewal

How Christ changes all of life

Keswick 2010

Edited by Ali Hull

16 15 14 13 12 11 10   7 6 5 4 3 2 1

First published 2010 by Authentic Media Limited
Presley Way, Crownhill, Milton Keynes, Bucks., MK8 0ES
www.authenticmedia.co.uk

British Library Cataloguing in Publication Data

A catalogue record for this book is available from the
British Library

ISBN 978-1-85078-931-4

Cover design by David Smart
Photographs by Neil Edbrooke and Sam Townshend
Printed and bound in the UK by Cox and Wyman, Reading

Contents

Introduction by the Chairman of the 2010 Convention

I am often in countries which are very religious. Without exception, as I look at idols and road-side shrines and the demanding religious duties on the faithful, I always feel profoundly grateful that, in the Christian faith, we are able to enjoy the free and privileged access of children to their heavenly Father. It is a profound relationship with a holy and eternal God, mediated through all that Jesus Christ has done.

But sadly, one of the greatest challenges to Christian mission in our continent is 'nominal' or 'notional Christianity'. In almost every country across Europe, a very high percentage of each population ticks the box for 'Christian', whether Protestant, Catholic or Orthodox, but very low percentages are actively engaged in church life or show any serious commitment in their Christian discipleship. It is a form of religion which claims to be Christian by virtue of tradition, family, culture or religious observance, but lacks what truly matters – a living union with Jesus Christ. For this is how the New Testament would want to define the word 'Christian': a Christian is someone who is united to Christ; a church is a community in which Christ is at the centre. Christianity *is Christ*.

It has to be said that we who claim to know Christ often feel that our Christianity can easily become institutionalised or routine, lacking in the spiritual vibrancy and devotion that we know is of the essence of living faith. So the 2010 Keswick theme was very timely: *Christ-centred renewal*. Some twelve thousand people – of varying ages, denominations, and cultures – gathered around God's word with this as their longing: to encounter the living Christ.

The history of the Convention has had this as its central aim: we seek renewal and refreshment as we meet Christ through the power of the word and Spirit. There are plenty of distractions in our busy lives which can dull our devotion, take the edge off our commitment, and gradually deaden our spiritual sensitivity. So just as the event itself brought refreshment to the thousands who attended, we hope that this selection of sermons will do the same for you, the reader.

May it encourage many of us around the world to listen carefully to God's word, so that it will enhance our experience of Christ's life and re-energise our commitment to serve him.

Jonathan Lamb
Chairman

The Bible Readings

What would Jesus say?

by Paul Mallard

Paul Mallard

Paul Mallard is the Director of Training and Development of the Midlands Gospel Partnership and former pastor of Woodgreen Evangelical Church in Worcester. He is zealous for teaching the Bible so that it is readily understood and applicable to life today. He believes that training a new generation of Christian leaders is very important and has been involved in a number of training programmes. He is married to Edrie; they have four children and two grandchildren. He has a great affection for Birmingham, where he was born and brought up, and is a keen West Bromwich Albion supporter.

1. Living and loving: Revelation 2:1–7

Introduction

We are going to look back into chapter 1, at the first vision of the exalted and glorified Christ, because this sets the tone for the letters that Jesus addresses to the churches in Revelation 2 and 3. Then we are going to look at the first letter, to the church at Ephesus. It is very clear, as you read through these New Testament letters, that the more you understand the background to the city where the church is placed, the better you can understand the letter that is written to it. So at the beginning of each Bible reading, I will give you that background.

John is on the island of Patmos, for the sake of the gospel, and while he is there, he hears a voice, sees a vision and receives a vocation. The vocation is to write to the seven churches of Asia Minor, in the eastern part of the Roman Empire, in what is now Turkey. The first letter is to Ephesus, because the first place the postman would arrive when he came from Patmos is Ephesus. Then the letters move round in a horseshoe, up from Patmos to Smyrna, to Pergamum and through Thyatira, Sardis, Philadelphia and finally to Laodicea.

The famous city of Ephesus

The city of Ephesus was a great city: the most important of these seven cities. It had a population of about a quarter of a million, which was a fabulous number in those days, and was nicknamed the Light of Asia. It was famous for its banks, buildings and wonderful boulevards. It had the best harbour in Asia. And it was also a melting pot: people came to Ephesus from all over the Roman Empire. There you would find Greeks, Jews, Romans, even Brits, and there is some evidence that people from as far away as India and even China were in the city of Ephesus, and so presumably in the church as well.

The wicked city

In Acts 19, when Paul is preaching at Ephesus, he comes into conflict with the makers of idols for the temple of Diana. This temple was a massive structure, one of the wonders of the world, five times bigger than the Parthenon in Athens. It had 127 columns, each over sixty feet high, and was a huge enterprise. People came from all over the world to engage in pagan worship there, and it was known for the occult. In those days, an Ephesian letter was not the letter of Paul: it was a magic spell, written by a sorcerer, to curse your enemy. It was a demon-infested city, when the gospel arrived, and it was also an immoral city.

The well-established church

In this dark place, this church shone as a light. It had been founded by the apostle Paul in around 52 AD as part of his third missionary journey, and he had spent two years there. It was probably from Ephesus that he sent out missionaries to plant other churches. Ten years later, Paul wrote the letter to the Ephesians, the crown of his theology. Timothy served the church at Ephesus as pastor, after Paul was imprisoned, and 1 and 2 Timothy were written to him while he was there. And, according to tradition, John the apostle, who wrote the book of Revelation, was the pastor of the church in Ephesus.

There is a wonderful story that when John was an old man, in his nineties, he would be carried on his bed into the church. The people would say to him, 'John, give us a word from the Lord.' He would say,

'Little children, love one another.' If only preachers could be so brief! That message is reflected in 1 John and it is one of the great themes in the Lord's letter to the church at Ephesus.

Turn to Revelation 2 and let me read verses 1 and 7 again. These are the brackets of the letter. This is how it begins: (v. 1) 'To the angel of the church in Ephesus write: These are the words . . .' Every one of the letters begins like that. Then (v. 7) 'He who has an ear, let him hear what the Spirit says to the churches.' Again, every one of the seven churches ends on that note.

What are the marks of being godly? One of the marks, and one of the needs of our spiritual renewal, is to be people who love the word of God. What we have in our hands is the most precious physical object in the Universe. This is the word of the living God. What the Scriptures say, God says. But the purpose of God in speaking to us is not simply to entertain, enthrall or even inform us. The purpose of the word of God is to transform us. If we are serious about Christ-centred renewal, then we must be serious about listening to the word of God. If we want to understand what God is saying to us, we must listen to the word, but then we have got to put it into practice.

We are talking about renewal this week. God the Father is the author of renewal. He chose us in Christ before the foundation of the world that we might be holy, and we should strive for holiness. That is God's plan and purpose for our lives. Jesus Christ is the model of renewal, to become like Jesus is the goal of our lives, and the Holy Spirit is the agent of renewal. As we go through these letters, every one of them speaks of the ministry of the Spirit: 'Hear what the Spirit is saying to the churches.' But the word of God is the instrument of renewal. If we are to be renewed in the power of God to be the kind of people that God wants us to be then we have to listen to what God says to us through his word.

The author

Who is the author of the book of Revelation? It is fairly obvious that it is the apostle John (Rev. 1:1). He introduces himself (vs. 4,9). The early church fathers were quite convinced that this is John the apostle, the son of Zebedee, the beloved disciple. John is an old man in a tough spot, probably in his nineties, and it is the end of the first century. The emperor on the throne is Domitian, and he has launched a persecution of the church that has put John on the island. You can imagine John pacing up and down on the island at night, looking across the sea to the cities on the shore, wondering, 'Does the church have a future?' As we look at our church at the beginning of the twenty-first century, we may ask that question: 'Does my church have a future?' (We will come back to this in the next chapter).

The vision of awesome majesty

It is into that situation suddenly that the Lord Jesus steps (v. 10): 'On the Lord's Day I was in the Spirit and I heard behind me a loud voice like a trumpet which said, "Write on a scroll what you see."' Although John is the writer of the letter, each of the letters come directly from the Lord Jesus. When we read the whole of the book of Revelation, it is Christ speaking to us, and the book begins with this vision of Christ, a vision of awesome majesty (Rev. 1:13–16). John can barely describe it, and he uses the word 'like' or 'as' seven times. And John says, 'When I saw him, I fell at his feet as if I was dead.' This is Jesus now, the awesome glorious majesty of Jesus now. He is not the babe of Bethlehem, the pale Galilean, the man of Calvary bathed in blood. He is king of kings and Lord of lords, the strong Son of God, and as the church goes through suffering and trial and difficulty, we need to see that Christ reigns.

He is magnificent, glorious and majestic, and there is an awesomeness about him. John falls at his feet as if he is dead. This is John the beloved disciple, yet as he looks at Jesus, there is a terrifying otherness. Liam was speaking last night about the terrible beauty of God and the law of God. When we look at Jesus, we see a terrible beauty. He is our friend, but he is not our mate, our pal. He is the Holy One of God.

At the end of the nineteenth century, the great Liberal prime minister Mr Gladstone was invited to speak to the Oxford Union and they gave him the subject, 'What do you think will happen in the twentieth century?' Being a Liberal, he was very optimistic, and said,

'Lots of wonderful things will happen in the twentieth century.' Then they asked him, 'Is there anything that you are anxious about?' Gladstone is said to have paused for a moment. Then he said, 'There is one thing that alarms me above everything else. Men and women are losing the fear of God.'

We live in a culture that has lost the fear of God, because the church has lost the fear of God. We no longer think of God as awesome, glorious and majestic. The Hebrew word for 'glory' means the heaviness of God. God is substantial, significant. We need to regain that sense of the awesome glory of Jesus, the magnificent warrior who will conquer his enemies and come for his people.

A vision of amazing mercy

Verse 17, '. . . he placed his right hand on me and said, "Do not be afraid. I am the first and I am the last."' Here is the Lord of glory, and there is John lying face down in the dirt. What does Jesus do? He stoops from his throne and he lifts up his servant. He is the glorious merciful Saviour who stoops from the glory of heaven to lift sinners out of the dirt and to put their feet on a rock. There is a wonderful verse in Psalm 4, where David refers to God as 'my glory and the lifter of my head'. It is a picture of the ancient court where a man who had offended the king would be thrown on his face. If the king decided that there would be no mercy, he would click his fingers and the man would be taken out for execution. If the king decided to have mercy, he might point to one of his officers and they would come and lift up the man's head so that the man could see the king. But if the king wanted to demonstrate his forgiveness to the one who had offended him, he would leave his throne and come to where the man was in the dirt and would lift up his head. The first face the man would see would be the face of the king.

The audience

To whom are these letters written? Verse 4 tells us they are the churches in Asia: Ephesus, Smyrna, Pergamum, Thyatira, Sardis,

Philadelphia and Laodicea. These are churches facing persecution, opposition, even meltdown, and yet the wonderful message of the letters is, 'I know exactly where you are.' Jesus says to each of them, 'I know your hopes and your dreams; your faults and your failings; your joys and your sorrows; your temptations and frustrations.' These churches were not so different from us.

The angels

Verse 1 of chapter 2 begins by referring to the angel of the church in Ephesus, and each of the letters begins in this way. Who is the angel? There has been all sorts of debate over this. They may be the guardian angels of the churches, or, in a general sense, the spirit of the ethos of the church. But, without being dogmatic, the most likely explanation is that they are the ministers of the churches: the pastors, the elders, the bishops. Because if you want to speak to a church, who do you speak to first? You speak to the leaders. So these letters are for the leaders, but they are also for individuals.

The aim

The purpose of the whole of the book of Revelation, and of the letters in particular, is to be a blessing to the people of God. That might come as a bit of a surprise. We have a fear of the book of Revelation, and we have the idea that you cannot possibly understand it unless you have been a Christian for forty years, with an IQ of 300 and a PhD in Applied Theology. But think about it: it is written to the churches and Christians who are going through troubles. At any moment, someone might be there to arrest them. Do you think the Lord is going to write, 'I know how difficult it is but, to take your mind off it, here is a puzzle to solve.' It is not a puzzle book, it is a picture book – what we call apocalyptic. It is speaking to us in pictures. When you look at a political cartoon, you know that the lion stands for England and the eagle stands for America. The book of Revelation works in the same way. It is thinking in pictures and the purpose is to encourage the people of God, to show what Christ is like and what his purposes are.

Disturbing the comfortable

Christians are comfortable people and sometimes the only way you can get us out of our apathy is to come in with words that are challenging. So for five out of the seven churches, Jesus has some hard things to say. He says those things because he loves the church and wants to reform and renew the church.

Comforting the disturbed

If we feel we are struggling, there are some wonderful words of comfort here. We are Christians living between the already and the not yet. We already have so many things in Christ. We are wealthy in Christ, we are seated in the heavenly realms with Christ, we have every spiritual blessing in Christ, but we are also at the same time struggling every day with sin, failure, doubt, illness, bereavement and those things that pull us away from the Lord. Jesus knows and he brings comfort by saying, 'I am with you and I am going to bring a new world, where there is no pain, no shame, no sorrow and no stain of evil.' The great theme of this book of Revelation, and every letter ends with it, is to lift up our eyes to see heaven. Jesus wants us to be optimistic, to realise that we are on the victory side. When we trusted in Christ, when we were placed in Christ, we were placed in that position of ultimate strength.

What is right with the church in Ephesus?

Look at verses 1 to 3 and then again at verse 6. What does he see when he looks at this church? He sees lots of good things (vs. 2,3):

A busy church

First of all, it is a busy church. Look at verse 2, 'I know your deeds, your hard work'. The Greek word there literally means 'labouring to the point of exhaustion.' And it is good to be a busy church. If you are saved, you are set aside for service. What's the role of a pastor/teacher? It is not to do the ministry but to prepare the saints for works of service. My task as a minister is to coach God's people so that they can be busy about the Lord's service. Every Christian has a gift which is given by Christ for the glory of God and for the building up of the church. Whoever you are, whatever gift you have, it is for the good of the church, and you are needed.

It is a bit like the difference between football and rugby. Have you ever watched an international football match and an international rugby match? There is a massive difference between the two. With a few exceptions, footballers are healthy young men of the same kind of shape: by and large they look the same. Whereas, in a rugby team, you can be any shape, any size, any fitness and you can be part of the team. So you have got the three guys on the front row who are square, and slightly brain-damaged, the guys in the second row who are about seven foot three and look like ostriches, the fly half and the scrum half who is about five foot and tiny, and then the guys at the back who are really fit and could do a ten second hundred metres. The church is like a rugby team: every shape, every size, every kind of gifting.

A discerning church

The church of Ephesus is a discerning church (v. 2) He talks in verse 2 of the false teachers, which comes up again in the letter to the church at Thyatira. Notice the vehemence of it: You cannot tolerate these false teachers in an age which loves tolerance. In verse 6 the sentiment is even stronger: 'You have this in your favour: you hate the practices of the Nicolaitans which I also hate.' Truth is important and this was a discerning church.

A steadfast church

Verse 3: 'You have persevered and have endured hardship for my name, and have not grown weary.' Ephesus is a church that went through persecution. It had seen its pastor, John, thrown into prison but it had not given up.

What is wrong with the church in Ephesus?

Your first love

This is a balanced church. There is a balance between truth and activity, steadfastness and ministry, faithfulness and vision. Yet (v. 5): 'Remember the height from which you have fallen. Repent and do the things you did at first. If you do not repent, I will come to you and remove your lampstand from its place.' There is something invisible but wrong at the heart of this church which threatens its future existence. What was wrong? 'You have forsaken your first love.' It must be one of the most devastating statements in the whole of Scripture. One person translates it like this: 'You do not love me as much as you used to. You have given up loving me.' When the church was planted in 52 AD, it had been on fire for God. When Paul wrote the letter to the Ephesians in 62 AD, about thirty years before, it was a church that had a reputation for love (Eph. 1:15; 6:24). But now that love has grown cold. You can imagine the Christians there saying, 'We are tired out in ministry. Haven't you seen our programme? We are fighting for the truth. We are willing to stand and suffer for your name.' 'Yes,' says the Lord, 'but you do not love me like you used to. You can have all those things but if your love has grown cold, then it is fatal.'

What are the infallible signs of losing our first love?

No passion for his presence

Have you noticed that lovers love to be alone? Even if there are lots of people around, they are still alone. When you love someone, you want to be with them. You want to listen to them, to listen to people talking about them. It is a busy church and busyness is not wrong but somehow perhaps they have lost that time in the presence of Christ. Sometimes we can be so busy about the Lord's service that we do not have time for the Lord we serve. The issue is worship.

Let me be a tad controversial. One of the things that the church has discovered over the last few years is that worship can be understood in a very broad sense. Worship is everything we do, it is 24/7 presenting our bodies as living sacrifices to God. We worship God in the office, in the factory, when we are looking after the kids, struggling with pain, dealing with demanding elderly relatives. We are worshipping God in the humdrum things. I believe the New Testament talked in that broad sense about worship but it also talked about those moments that we spend gazing on God. We come, as individuals or as the body of Christ, and spend time gazing on the beauty of the Lord, declaring his worth, delighting in his character, loving him, adoring him, honouring him, praising his name, surrendering our will to him.

We are destined for worship and there is something wonderful about preaching because preaching is not what you do after the worship. There is a circularity about worship; we speak to God in prayer and praise, God comes to us through his word, and when we sit under preaching it should be a divine encounter. What is my aim in preaching? It is to set before the people of God the bounty and the beauty of the Lord, so that they may say, 'Isn't Jesus wonderful?'

One of the most overwhelming things that ever strikes me is that God should call me to preach the gospel. I preach three or four times a week on average. I have preached between three and four thousand sermons, but there have been times in my ministry when I have lost that joy. What do you have to do then? Get back to the love of Christ and say, 'Why am I standing before God's people?' Not just because I love preaching but because I love Jesus.

In verse 4, we are assuming that the love that is spoken of here is a love for Christ, but it could equally be a love for God's people. When we fall out of love with the Lord, we find God's people very difficult. I delight in God's people, but some of them are quite difficult. In your church, you have got some people who are quite difficult. What is it that sustains a ministry of loving difficult people? The love of Christ: we cannot love the church unless we love Christ.

What is needed?

Verse 5, 'Remember the height from which you have fallen. Repent and do the things that you did at first.' The Greek tense means 'keep on' remembering – bring it to mind and hold it there. Remember when you first became a Christian. Remember how you fell in love with Jesus. Remember it, keep dwelling on it. Are you still thrilled to be a Christian? Are you still amazed that God could save you? Go back to the cross.

The tense of the verb for repent is different. It is a sudden turning, an urgent thing, one and for all. And then he says 'return' – return to where you were. Remember when you first fell in love with Jesus, remember when you first went to the cross? Go back to that point. Go back to the primitive unsophisticated simplicity of that first love.

I was converted when I was eleven. My dad worked in a factory, my mum worked in a shop, and at the age of eighteen, I went to study theology at Cambridge University. I was terrified, so I said to our youth leader, 'What must I do?' and he said 'The moment you go there, make it clear you love Jesus.' This was the 1970s. Can you remember all those garish little round stickers? They were red and green and yellow, and said 'Smile Jesus loves you.' I plastered my suitcase, my books and my clothes with them. I looked like a set of traffic lights. I would not dream of doing that now; I am much too sophisticated. But there are times when I have longed to have that lack of sophistication that comes when you fall in love.

I am not suggesting that we become weird but are we willing to go back to that simplicity that we once had? He gives them two encouragements to do so. One is negative and one is positive. The negative one in verse 5 – if you do not do something about it you have no future. The positive one, in verse 7, is a promise of paradise. The word paradise is used three times in the New Testament. It is used when Jesus is speaking to the thief on the cross, and Paul uses it in 2 Corinthians 12. It is a Persian word that refers to a garden of delight. How do I get this first love back? The way to get back that first love is not to work hard at it, it is to look at his love for you.

I have a wonderfully patient wife. In spite of all the suffering that she has to go through, she is immensely loyal and the more I look at her love, the more my heart beats with love for her. But in a greater way, in a more wonderful way, if we are to love Christ as we should, we have to look at his love for us. There was a great Bible teacher known as Professor Duncan, and he was an expert in the Hebrew of the Old Testament. One day he was lecturing on Isaiah and he got to the verse, in Hebrew, 'All we like sheep have gone astray and we've turned every one to his own way but the Lord has laid on him the iniquity of us all.' As he began to expound this verse to his students, suddenly he stopped and he could not speak. The words would not come. After a couple of minutes, he spoke through tears, in a breaking voice: 'It was damnation, it was hell, and he took it for us.' When was the last time you saw that Calvary love and it broke your heart and it showed you how much you love your Saviour?

2. Revelation and reality: Revelation 3:1–13

Introduction

We have been looking at this great theme of Christ-centred renewal and, as we have looked at each of the churches, we have picked up particular messages to help us to be the kind of men and women, and the kind of transformed churches, that God wants us to be. We come this morning to two churches that are a study in contrasts. On the outside, they look very different, and the Lord's assessment of them was very different as well.

The city of Sardis

Sardis had been a rich, commercial city, where King Croesus lived. King Croesus was incredibly rich – there used to be a phrase, 'as rich as Croesus'. Gold had been discovered in Sardis and it was the first place in the world to mint gold coins. It had been a city of luxury and pleasure – but that was six hundred years before the events that we are reading about. It had also thought of itself as impregnable. Sardis was built on a huge mount, with its citadel on the top, and twice in its history, the guards at the doors of the citadel had thought they were so invincible, they had gone to sleep. Then their enemies came through the gates and conquered the city. Jesus says to the church, 'Wake up and shape up, because you are in a serious condition!'

Sardis was also a city whose glory had faded. The old days of riches were long gone. There had been an earthquake, in 17 AD, and the city had never recovered. Many of the buildings had crumbled, some of the shops were boarded over. There had also been an attempt to build a temple to Diana, that would rival the temple in Ephesus, and it had never been finished. The church was like that: Jesus said to the church,

'You're great at beginnings but you do not finish. You have got no per-severance.'

The city of Philadelphia

Philadelphia was the youngest of the seven cities, and in fact it had been set up as a missionary city. That might sound strange, but when Alexander the Great conquered the ancient world, he wanted to spread the religion of Hellenism, Greek culture and a Greek way of thinking, to the barbarians. The only way to cement the empire together was to get the enemies speaking Greek, thinking Greek, and so on. So Philadelphia was a missionary city with a Hellenistic gospel. It was also a small city and, like Sardis, it had suffered during the earth-quake in 17 AD. It had never really got the population back, and that was probably why the church was so small. It also had a strong Jewish community. Remember, all the early Christians were Jews, and they had been thrown out of the synagogue. Jesus says to them, 'They might have shut the door at the synagogue, but I am going to open a door of opportunity and ministry, so that you can take out the gospel.'

Does the church have a future?

Keep your finger in Revelation 3 and turn over to chapter 7. We need to understand that the letters and the promises to the churches do not end at the end of chapter 3. The whole book of Revelation is written to encourage these churches, as they face the devil, false teaching and persecution. Those things come up later in Revelation 12 and 13. We see the dragon, and the two henchmen of the dragon, that represent persecution and false teaching. Later on in the book we read about the whore of Babylon, which represents the seductions of this world that are always trying to drag the church away from what the church should be.

These are the things that the early church is facing, and John is on Patmos, for the sake of the gospel, and in his mind, the question must be, 'Does the church have a future? Can there be a future for this church?' So what the Lord does in many of these chapters is to remind John the church has a wonderful future. He will build his church and the gates of hell will not prevail against it, and that is what we read about in chapter 7. Remember the wonderful parable of the mustard seed. When it starts, you can barely see it, but then it grows into this tree that is so massive, all the birds can come and live in it. That is what the kingdom of God is like. It is so tiny in the beginning, but it is going to grow. The church is so tiny, but it is going to grow, and this is the great message Jesus is giving John – and to us today.

Here's a very different question. Does *my* church have a future? Jesus guarantees the future of the church, but he does not guarantee the future of any *particular* church or denomination. History is littered with churches and denominations that have been strong in the past, but have now lost the gospel and are dead or dying. And the big question that we have to ask is, Does my church have a future?

The churches of Sardis and Philadelphia looked entirely different. The church at Sardis was the big church, that everybody flocked to: the church with a tremendous history. The church at Philadelphia was small and struggling: it didn't have many people and its back was against the wall. And that is what it would have looked like. You'd have got in your car and driven straight past Philadelphia to go to Sardis, because that was the church to be at, but Jesus said something very different. 'To the church at Sardis,' he says, 'you have got a great history but a doubtful future.' To the church at Philadelphia, he says, 'You have got a struggling present but a glorious future. I am going to open the door of ministry to you.' As we look at these two churches, we are going to learn some important lessons about what a church needs to be and to do, under God, to have a future.

The church at Sardis: a diagnosis (Rev. 3:1–3)

Every one of the letters so far has begun with a commendation. Jesus has always found something good to say to the church. With Sardis, there is nothing good. Something slightly good comes a bit later but, at this point, there is nothing good. The diagnosis of the church is given in verses 1 to 3, and there are two things to note: a serious condition and a radical solution.

A serious condition (v. 1)

Sardis was the kind of church that you would put in your top ten. It was the kind of church that, if you are a pastor and you get a phone call from the church secretary at Sardis, and he says, 'This summer our pastor is away, will you come and preach at the church at Sardis?' you would say, 'I have made it. I am preaching at Sardis in August!' It had a fantastic reputation but look at what the Lord says. In reality, there is a form of godliness but there is no power. Have you seen the pictures of those bodies that they have dug up from peat bogs in Denmark? People fell into bogs and were, by some mystery of chemistry, perfectly preserved. You can see the pictures. They look perfectly preserved and yet they are profoundly dead. That is what this church is like.

How do you get to be like that? Look again in verse 1. What does the Lord mention right at the beginning? These introductions always fit in with the nature of the church: 'He is the one who holds the seven spirits in his right hand.' What is physical death? Physical death is when the spirit leaves the body. Death in a church is the absence of the Holy Spirit. The life of the church is the life of the Holy Spirit.

Incidentally, seven spirits does not mean there are seven Holy Spirits. This is a book of symbols, and seven is a symbol of perfection. The perfection of the living Spirit of God is in the hand of Jesus, because Jesus, in his ascension, pours the Spirit upon the church. He has poured the Spirit on the church, and the church has been consumed and changed by the fire of God. At Sardis, they have forgotten that we can do nothing, nothing, without the power of the Holy Spirit. I do not know what your theology is, when it comes to the doctrine of the Holy Spirit, but let me tell you this. If your theology does not put you in a position where, every day, you are crying to God for the life of his Spirit to come and invade his church, then you need to change your theology. If you have a theology that says 'We have got everything and we are fine', then you need to change your theology, because in our nation we are in desperate need. If you look at our nation today and you think that this is spiritual health, then you do not know what spiritual health looks like.

I am not a charismatic. I love charismatics, I preach in charismatic churches, I preach in Pentecostal churches, they are my dearest brothers in Christ. I do not put myself under that label, but I share that longing for God to manifest his presence amongst his people in preaching. Preaching is not just teaching, it is an event where God comes. You can never quite explain it because, when the Spirit comes, the Spirit comes. And you cannot explain the inexplicable. The Holy Spirit is in the hand of Christ, and Jesus said, 'I will pour my Spirit on the church.' We need him. The church in Sardis was in a dangerous position and it needed a radical answer.

A radical solution (vs. 2,3)

Verse 2 says 'Wake up, strengthen what remains' and verse 3 says, 'Shape up. It is a serious condition you are in and you need to do something about it.' Have you ever seen the programme *Casualty*? We have a very clear programme on a Saturday night, in our house. My wife sits down to watch *Casualty* and I go to bed. I need to get up really early in the morning and pray and get ready, but that is not the real reason. I cannot stand *Casualty*. It terrifies me. Any minute, something bad is going to happen. A man with a lawnmower, somebody's going to lose a foot. But even that isn't the bad bit. There is always that moment where the body's there and the doctor says 'Oh, he has gone.' Then somebody else says, 'No, there is a spark of life there!' They get one of these needles and plunge it into the chest, and they get these horrible electric things . . . Because the only thing that brings you back from the very brink is something radical. That is exactly what Jesus is saying to these churches. He may be saying that to your church. 'You're sleepwalking into death, so wake up and strengthen the things that remain!'

The church at Sardis was depending on their past reputation. It had a wonderful past reputation, but that was the past. Shall I tell you one of the signs of a dying church? It is wedded to its tradition and its nostalgia, and it has no vision for the future. It is great to learn from the past but we cannot dwell in the past. The past is supposed to inspire us: it is not supposed to paralyse us, and if we do not change, we die. And change is tough in church life, it really is tough. We never change the gospel, we cannot change the gospel, the gospel is not ours to change, but a lot of other things we have to change. Because if you do not change, you have death.

I really love cemeteries, I find a cemetery, I sit there and I read deep theology books. Do you know what I like about cemeteries? They're so quiet. But you imagine trying to read the same book amongst your parent and toddlers group at church. We have three parent and toddlers groups at my church in Worcester and they scare me to death. I never go in because I cannot cope. You have kids running all over the place, mums feeding, babies, snotty noses – it is terrible! But it is life. Some of our churches look like graveyards. And some churches look like parent and toddler meetings. There is life and it is not comfortable. It was never meant to be comfortable! Woe betide any church when it gets comfortable. Wake up!

You need to do something serious if you are to have life. And where the Spirit of God is, there is amazing life. The Spirit of God is the agent of God. Whatever God does in this world, the Holy Spirit is the agent. So creation is the work of the Spirit. He brooded over the depths. He renews the creation. In the book of Job, it says he garnishes the heavens. You know what garnish is, it is that special bit you put on your food. New life is the work of the Spirit. It is not easy and it is not comfortable.

Shape up!

'Shape up, deal with the issues in your church. Repent.' The single most important aspect of the doctrine of the ministry and work of the Person of the Holy Spirit, that as Christians we neglect, is not the filling or the baptism of the Spirit. It is the fact that the Holy Spirit is a divine Person, co-equal and co-eternal with the Father and the Son. God is three and God is one and the Father is God and the Son is God and the Holy Spirit is God. He is a Person. People who should know better often refer to the Holy Spirit as 'It.' The Holy Spirit is a gentle, godly, holy Spirit. In Ephesians 4:30, Paul talks about grieving the Spirit. That is a love word. It does not even say 'Don't anger the Spirit.' What grieves the Spirit? Bitterness.

I remember a pastor friend of mine said, 'I need some advice. I have discovered that in the church there are two Christian brothers who won't talk to one another. I have been to one of them and said, "Will you meet with your brother?" and he said, "Yes." I went to the other one and I said, "Will you meet with your brother?" and he said, "No." So I said, "This is important, because all the church knows about it. The future of this church depends on it." And the man said, "I'd rather the church die than go and talk to that man." ' And I said to that pastor, 'You should discipline him. If he will not sit down with his brother, you have got to deal with it. If you do not, it will kill your church. If you do not do something, then Jesus will.' Jesus says to the church in Sardis, 'If you do not do something, the presence of the Spirit will dissipate, it will be gone. I will come like a thief and you will have no future at all.'

As the church of Jesus Christ, and as individual Christians, we need regularly, daily, to be filled with the Holy Spirit. The filling of the Spirit is an ongoing daily thing. 'Keep being filled', says the apostle Paul. It is not like we come to this little fountain with the cup of our life and we fill this little cup. We come with the cup of our life to a thousand Niagara Falls. We say, 'Lord fill me today, because I need you. I have got a difficult place of work and I have got difficult relations. I do not know how my marriage is going to work and I do not know how to witness to you. I do not know how to preach and I do not know how to cope – fill me.' And guess what happens? This great ocean of the fullness of the Spirit comes into our lives and flows over. Every moment of every day we need to be crying 'Oh God, send your Spirit.' How many of you pray for your preacher, every Sunday, that God may fill him with the Spirit? Preaching is not just conveying information: preaching is a divine event, and a preacher needs the power of the Spirit of the living God.

The prognosis (vs. 4–6)

The one good thing about this church is that not everybody had succumbed to death (v. 4). The church was in a state of compromise but there were some who were different. These people are known to God. Notice the key significance of these people: they are dressed in white robes. What did the white robes signify? They were a symbol in those days of festivity: when you were going to have a celebration, you put on white robes. They were robes of victory, they were robes of purity; most of all they were robes at a wedding. When a Roman went to a wedding, he put on a white toga, just as a bride today puts on a white dress. But it is more than that.

White robes are a symbol, in John's thinking, of the righteousness of Christ. This is talking about this glorious doctrine of justification by faith. We are clothed in the righteousness of Jesus. Justification is not the work of God *in* us, it is the work of God *for* us, it is a declaration that God sees us as righteous in his sight because we are clothed in the pure and perfect righteousness of Christ. God justifies the ungodly. God blots out sin, and God does not want you to remember what he has chosen to forget.

Nor is that all that justification is. It does not go far enough. Justification is a positive thing. He takes the righteousness of Christ and he covers us with it. He who had no sin was made sin for us, that we might become the righteousness of Christ. Remember when Jesus came out of the waters of baptism? His Father looks at him and says 'This is my beloved Son, with whom I am well pleased.' I am pleased with his perfect righteousness and his utter obedience. Those robes of righteousness are laid on your shoulders today and when God looks at you, he sees the glorious righteousness of Jesus. You are as right with God as you ever can be. It is instantaneous, it is legal, it is declarative and it is glorious. It is the gospel.

What do you do with a dying church? What are the two things that are there in the text? They are the Holy Spirit and the doctrine of justification by faith. If you are the pastor of a dying church today, depend on the Holy Spirit and preach justification by faith. When you are in the pulpit, preach your heart out as if it all depended on you. When you get down on your knees, pray to God and recognise that it all depends on him. That is the church at Sardis.

The church at Philadelphia

Philadelphia is about thirty miles down the road and it is very different. The one big message to Philadelphia (v. 11) is 'Don't quit.' Look at the diagnosis in verses 8 and 10. This is a church, first of all, that had little strength. It is not a strong, big church, it is probably struggling. Maybe that is what your church is doing – struggling. It is great to come here, but on Sunday, you have to to go back to your little fellowship, and it is not easy.

In my first church, my wife and I were the youngest couple there, and in the first year of my ministry, I really changed that church. Eleven people died and one person got converted. You cannot sustain a ministry on that for long. The second year was not much better. I would come to conferences like this and go back feeling guilty and intimidated. Sometimes pastors feel like that. Actually I love going to small churches these days because God is blessing them. Look at what else he says: 'You're wonderfully faithful. You may be small and you may not have much strength but you have kept my word, you haven't denied me, you have kept my word to endure.'

I was preaching last week in an Asian fellowship in Birmingham. I have been preaching there over a number of years. It has been a small church, but it is growing. When I first went, it was just Asian guys, but last week, now they have Asian guys and black guys and white guys. God is working there because they are faithful. Their pastor goes into Muslim areas and preaches Christ, and they do not like that. But he just keeps going. They're faithful.

What does the Lord demand of us? He demands that we are faithful. Sometimes we think 'faithful' means 'never changing'. It does not. Being faithful to God and faithful in the church sometimes does mean changing. It also means being obedient, carrying on and not giving up. You know that is what God loves and commends. That is why he has no criticism at all, for this church, like the church in Smyrna. The Lord is just pleased with his church and he puts an open door in front of them.

Have you heard of John Akhwari? He was a runner in the Olympic Games, who came to Mexico to run in the marathon. He had badly damaged his leg and it was painful just to put his foot to the ground but he wouldn't give up, and lots of people cheered him as he finished. Afterwards they said to him, 'Why on earth did you carry on?' You know what he said? 'My country didn't send me to

Paul Mallard

start a race. My country sent me to finish a race.' That is faithfulness, isn't it?

If you feel like giving up, you are in good company. Moses felt like giving up. He was the pastor of two million people. He said, 'Lord, I cannot do it any more.' Elijah felt like giving up and Jeremiah felt like giving up. Even Paul felt like giving up, in 2 Corinthians. When you feel like giving up and you are in the position where you are just hanging on to God, God can bless you. Because when you are weak, you are strong.

One day when my wife was particularly unwell, there was a week when we were up all night with pain. I had to preach on Sunday and it was a hot day. I thought 'How am I going to preach today?' In every church I have been, I have held a surgery once a week where people can come and ask questions and pray. There is a dear godly lady called Ettie and she used to come in to the surgery and she'd say 'Pray for Ernie' (that was her husband) 'because he just does not want to know anything about Jesus.' I prayed for him and he never came to church – except on this day when I felt so rotten.

I stood in the pulpit and it felt as if my mouth was filled with rocks. My knees were quaking and I do not know what I preached. I am not exaggerating, I just talked. I finished and I said to my wife, 'I am not going to be a minister. I am not going to be a pastor any more. I am a total total failure.' I went home and I was depressed for three days. On Wednesday morning, I thought, I am going to give a bunch of flowers to Ettie and say, 'I am so sorry.' There was a knock on the door and it was Ernie. He says 'I'd like to talk to you about what you said on Sunday.' And I said, 'Remind me what I said on Sunday!'

Actually he just repeated the gospel, which I was thrilled about, because when you go on to automatic mode, what you love comes out. I had preached Christ. So he said 'Can I become a Christian?' and I said, 'You can' and I led him to Christ. He died about eighteen months after that. When you are weak, you are strong. That is what Jesus is saying to the church in Philadelphia: 'You are faithful. I will keep you.'

Three encouragements to the church

A present opportunity (v. 7)

In the hands of Jesus is the key of David. He lays before the church a wonderful opportunity. Wherever you are spiritually, wherever you are physically, whatever your trials and troubles and heartbreaks can be, Jesus can offer a door of opportunity for you. Even in the midst of your suffering, Jesus can bring you to a place where he can bless you and he can use you.

I will never forget hearing Warren Wiersbe say that, in his first church, he was preaching one Sunday and he noticed a lady who had not been able to come for a number of Sundays because she was suffering the most tremendous suffering. Her husband was desperately ill and she was losing her sight. He said to her, 'Mary, I want you to know I am praying for you.' And she said, 'Thank you Pastor, what you praying for?' You're not expected to ask that, are you? He said he mumbled a few things and she said 'Pastor, shall I tell you what to pray for? Pray that I do not waste this suffering.'

In the midst of suffering, God opens the door for ministry. I have found a thousand times in my ministry that the experiences that my wife and I have wept over together, and the breaking and the bruising that the Lord has done in our lives, have provided tremendous opportunities for ministry. I would not be without them

A public vindication (v. 9)

Here is the second blessing that he gives to this church – a public vindication, verse 9. 'I will make those who are of the synagogue of Satan who claim to be Jews though they are not but are liars, I will make them come and fall down at your feet and acknowledge that I have loved you.' Some people acknowledge that this is the end of time. I suspect that it might mean that but it may also mean that those who are their worst enemies will become their dearest friends. God will convert these people. God is in the habit of converting his enemies and making his enemies his friends. He did it with me and with you.

A permanent reward (v. 11)

In our Western world, we are so sophisticated. We know Jesus is coming back, but we do not take it seriously. If you are in a struggling situation in a struggling church, do not give up. I want to close this morning with a word of personal testimony. I became a Christian in 1967. My mum and dad were the best mum and dad in the world but they knew nothing about God. The day I became a Christian, I started praying for my dad and my mum and my sister, and I said, 'God I cannot live if they are not saved. I cannot cope if they are not saved. Please save them.' Every day I prayed.

When I was eighteen, at university, my dad came to see me and I gave him a Christian text, and a Christian book. He wrote me a letter a few days later and said, 'I read that book you gave me and I went up in the bedroom. I got down on my knees and I asked Jesus to be my Saviour.' My dad became a man of God.

Then for thirty years nothing happened. I prayed every day for my sister and my mum, thirty years. Thirty years later my son, who was in Birmingham, rang me up and said, 'Dad, you better sit down. Aunt Julie, your sister, came to see me yesterday and she wants me to do a Bible study. She wants to become a Christian.' And now my sister was baptised but my mum's not interested and she does not want to know. She got harder and harder and then, about eighteen months ago, she was seriously ill. I sat by my mum and I held her hand and I said 'Mum, do you know where Dad is?' and she said 'Yes, he is in heaven.' And I said, 'Mum, do you know how to get to heaven?' and she said, 'No.' And I said, 'Mum, do you want me to tell you how to get to heaven?' and she said, 'Yes please.' I told her about Jesus and when I finished, she said, 'Please pray with me.' I held my mum's hand and I led her to Christ.

Then God did something amazing, because he made her better. She is still in a wheelchair but three Sundays later she went to the church and she has not stopped going to church since. Some of you are praying for your loved ones. I prayed for forty-one years. God heard those prayers.

In the dark days of the war Winston Churchill was asked to go to his old school, Harrow and give the speech at prize day. He was busy so he gave a speech that consisted of just seven words: 'Never never never never never give up.'

Life in the Spirit

by Alistair Begg

Alistair Begg

Alistair Begg is the senior minister of Parkside Church in suburban Cleveland, Ohio, where he has served since 1983. His teaching is heard daily across the USA on over one thousand radio stations that air the programme, 'Truth For Life'. He has written a number of books, as well as a revision of Spurgeon's devotional, *Morning and Evening*. He has been married to Susan for 34 years and they are the parents of three adult children.

Life in the Spirit 1: Romans 8

Introduction

It is the Holy Spirit who helps us in our weakness, a weakness that is readily apparent when we bow before God in prayer. Having considered a creation that groans, and a church that groans, now we are brought face to face with the wonder of wonders: a God who groans. Christopher Ash, in a wonderful little sentence, says, 'The wonder is that beneath our groanings there is the groaning of God praying to God.'

I would like to take a purposeful pause in this matter of weakness. It is important for us to recognise how much the Bible has to say about weakness and yet, despite that fact, so many of our protestations are in denial of what we know to be the case. Paul tells us 'when I am weak, then I am strong'. In my experience of weakness, he says, I have discovered the strength of God. If dependence is the objective, then weakness is actually an advantage. Yet our culture, both secular and Christian, encourages us to challenge that very notion.

An American commentator, Peggy Noonan, made this comment: 'For thirty years the self-esteem movement told the young they are perfect in every way. It is yielding something new in history – an entire generation with no proper sense of inadequacy.' Yet when we read the lives of those who have been most effective under God, we do not have to read too far in their biography to discover that their weakness was their strength. John Thornton wrote to Charles Simeon, as follows: 'Watch continually over your own spirit, and do all in love. We must grow downward in humility to soar heavenward.' Simeon was greatly used of God. It is the kind of word that we might so easily move quickly over. Paul, in 2 Corinthians 12, identifies the fact that God in the sovereignty of his purposes, in order to keep him from becoming conceited, gave him a thorn in the flesh. Elsewhere in that second letter, it is no surprise to find him saying, 'Who is sufficient for these things? We are not sufficient in ourselves, our sufficiency is from God' (2 Cor. 3:5).

In 2 Chronicles 20, we have a wonderful picture of the great and illustrious king Jehoshaphat. Jehoshaphat is overwhelmed and he turns to God in prayer, 'We have no power to face this vast army that is attacking us. We do not know what to do, but our eyes are upon you' (2 Chr. 20:12). This is not what we expect from leaders. It is an amazing picture of inadequacy, weakness and helplessness. Notice in verse 14, the very next phrase, 'Then the Spirit of the LORD came' and I will leave you to read the rest yourself.

The Spirit intercedes

This is always God's way. Romans 8:26, 'In the same way the Spirit helps us in our weakness.' He is the one who comes to help us in the face of 'the mortal ills that prevail', as Luther put it in his great hymn. How is it that the Spirit helps us? We are told that he intercedes for us. We do not know what we ought to pray for, but the Spirit intercedes for us. We have two members of the Trinity engaged in intercession, and what Christ does for us in heaven, Paul tells us, the Holy Spirit does for us in our hearts. As we saw in our earlier study, (v. 15), when all we can get out of our mourning or in the immediacy of some circumstance that has overwhelmed us, is 'Father', then miraculously and wonderfully that the Spirit steps in and intercedes with wordless groanings. It is not simply that the words cannot be expressed, it is that the words themselves are inexpressible.

There is something mysterious about all of this. It appears that the desires and the groans are ours, but they are not ours alone and apart from God's Spirit. They are his insofar as they are worked in us by him. In the most simplistic terms, it appears that what Paul is telling us is that the Spirit says, 'Father, this is what Begg is trying to say. Let me intercede on his behalf.' Notice that the Spirit's intercession is in accordance with the will of God. Psalm 139 says: 'Lord, you have searched me and you know me. You know when I sit down, when I stand up. You know the words of my mouth before I even speak them. Such knowledge is wonderful, I cannot attain to it.' When the Father searches the heart and encounters our unuttered groans, insofar as they are the intercessions of the Holy Spirit, those unuttered groans are a perfect reflection of the Father's own loving purpose. That is why there is something that takes us into the realm of mystery.

I confess that when I read this and reread it and thought about it, I was bereft of any kind of metaphor or analogy that would do any justice to it. I think the closest I could possibly come, and this is on the borders of it, is when a mother explains to us what her child is saying, by means of their inarticulate cooings. It is as if God bends down into the cradle of our lives and the Spirit of God interprets what is going on in our hearts. But this analogy does not come close to what is being expressed here. 'The guarantee of the answer to our prayers,' says Calvin, 'is found in the nature of their origins. God thoroughly approves of our desires as the thoughts of his own Spirit. Our heavenly Father will not refuse to satisfy yearnings, which by his own Spirit he has put within us.'

There is one sense in which verses 26 and 27 would have fitted better at the end of yesterday but we had no time. The mention of the Spirit interceding for the saints in accordance with God's will leads Paul on to address the will of God and the purposes of God, from all eternity. He is going to make it clear to his readers that the good work that God has begun in the lives of those who are in Christ Jesus (Rom. 8:1), he will bring to completion at the day of Christ Jesus (Phil. 1:6). And he reminds his readers of this in contrast to all the things that we do not know.

Wilson says this is not the language of tentative conjecture, but the language of experimental certainty. Paul is not an arm's-length theologian. He has taken all of the events of his life, the good, the bad and the ugly, and he puts them within the theological framework of the loving purpose of God who from all of eternity has been at work. This is not the believer simply saying, 'Don't worry, it will all work out for us somehow in the end.' It is something far deeper and more significant. Paul is saying that God is at work in all things for the good of his children.

The identity of the children

Who are these people then in whose lives God is at work? He is at work in the lives of those who love him, the ones who are loving God. One of the distinguishing features of being a Christian is that we love God. This was the distinguishing feature of the people of Israel in the Old Testament; the significance of the Shema which is said morning and evening in the homes of orthodox Jews throughout the world. Their fear of God is a filial fear. It is not servile; their love is expressive of intimacy but it is also in the awareness of the awesomeness, that we might ever say that the God who created the entire Universe is personally interested in the affairs of our lives. So much so, that even the things that we cannot give voice to, he pays attention to and answers.

This love that God's people have for him is based upon the initiative of his love towards them. Some people apparently stumble over this, I am not sure why. Paul is going to tell us here: 'I found a friend, oh such a friend, he loved me ere I knew him; he drew me with the cords of love and thus he bound me to him; and round my heart, so closely twined, these ties that nothing can sever, for I am his and he is mine, for ever and for ever.'

Working together for good

'All things work together for good', that is what it says in the King James Version. I do not think that is as good a translation as the NIV:

'and we know that in all things God works for good.' All things work together for good sounds as though the jigsaw puzzle pieces of life automatically jiggle themselves back into position. But, in actual fact, things do not work: it is God who is at work. He knows the big picture, he paints the big picture, and in the mystery of his purposes he works all things for the ultimate good of his children. This is so hard to get our tiny minds around, when we think of the disappointments of life.

If we want a cross-reference from this, we should read the story of Joseph, and read there how the activity of his father, the animosity of his brothers, the activity of the slave traders; all these things worked themselves out until eventually Joseph says, 'Remember, you intended this for evil, but God intended it for good.'

In verses 29 and 30, Paul unpacks God's purpose. He provides for us essentially an unbreakable chain of events. When you read 29 and 30, it is probably good to precede your reading of 29 and 30 with the doxology that comes at the end of chapter 11, and then when you have done your study, go back to the end of 11 again. That is the baseline from which we consider these things.

Those who he foreknew (v. 29)

Here is the first link in the chain. Does this mean, as some suggest, that God foreknew those who would believe? Yes, because God foresees everything that comes to pass. But is that all that Paul is saying? Certainly not. For the knowledge here of which he speaks is not so much factual knowledge as it is relational knowledge. In Exodus, it says 'You only have I known of all the families of the earth', and the NIV translates 'known' as 'chosen'. The idea is to return to the hymn verse: 'He loved me before I knew him.'

'He also then predestined them'. It is God's unerring purpose to put together a people that are his very own, an immeasurable company from every tribe and nation and people and tongue, and it is the utterly undeserved privilege of all who believe, to be included in that company. We have already noted the way in which Paul, having expounded this theme in the beginning of Ephesians, reminds the Ephesian believers how it was that the eternal purpose of God was worked out in their lives. Having scanned the heights, as it were, of God's predestinating will, he says

> in him we were also chosen, having been predestined according to the plan of him who works out everything in conformity with the purpose of his will in order that we, who were the first to hope in Christ, might be for the praise of his glory. And you also were included in Christ when you heard the word of truth, the gospel of your salvation, and having believed, you were marked in him with a seal, the promised Holy Spirit, who is a deposit guaranteeing our inheritance until the redemption of those who are God's possession to the praise of his glory.

He is using the very same terminology to make the point that God foreordains salvation but he also foreordains the means whereby men and women come to salvation. God does not believe for us. We believe.

We all believe this. You only need to go to a prayer meeting at any local church and you will find that everyone believes this. One brother or sister will say, 'Gracious God, how I thank you for opening my eyes and opening my ears. Were it not for your grace and goodness, I would be blind and deaf to your truth, and I thank you.' Not long after, someone will say, 'As we thank you for our salvation, we pray now for the salvation of those to whom we are going in our outreach. Teach me, Lord, what to say, for friends of mine are lost in sin. Lord Jesus Christ, I can plant and I can water but only you can make things grow.' It is this and more that is wrapped up in this terminology.

In 1984 Eric Alexander had the privilege of giving the Bible readings at the Urbana Missionary Conference in Illinois and I went. I had only been in the States twelve months, and I was glad to be in the company of anybody that represented home, not least of all him, and I trailed around behind him and listened carefully as he expounded Ephesians 1 to 3. When he came to this issue of predestination and the doctrine of election, he said, 'The doctrine of election is not a banner under which we march. Nor is it a bomb which we drop on the heads of men and women. But it is a bastion for the souls of men and women,' For the purpose of God in this work is not so that we will become articulate theologians. God's purpose in foreknowledge and predestination is to conform us to the likeness of his Son, so that the Lord Jesus Christ might be the firstborn among many brothers. The ultimate end of the divine decree is the exultation of the Lord Jesus Christ. It is never about us. It is always about him.

He also called

'Those God predestined, he also called'. He called by means of the preaching of the gospel. On the crest of the wave of divine sovereignty, the summons to men and women to believe rings out. It is a real summons; what theologians refer to as the free offer of the gospel, reminding those to whom we go that, whoever comes to Jesus, he will 'in no wise turn away'. For, as we said earlier, all that Christ has done for us is of no value to us so long as we remain outside of Christ.

Professor John Murray was having a parley with someone driving in a car in the Highlands and he asked his driver, 'What's the difference between preaching and a lecture?' His driver, the travelling companion, made several good stabs at it, but Murray kept saying, 'No, you still haven't got it.' Eventually, the driver said, 'What is it?' and Murray said, 'Preaching is a personal passionate plea. We beseech you, on Christ's behalf, be reconciled to God.'

Jonathan Edwards, who is often held up as one who had challenged such notions, believed that it was past all contradiction 'that Christ died to give an opportunity to all to be saved.' In that free offer of the gospel, it is the effectual call of God which raises men and women from death to life, which opens their eyes and unstops their ears. But that effectual call of God is not countermanding the unwillingness of an individual to believe. When you get in conversations like this, there are always two caricatures that you will never find in the Bible: the person who wants desperately to believe but isn't allowed to, and the person who desperately does not want to believe and has to. Those are not in the Bible, and we cannot squeeze them out of what Paul is saying here. Truths that look contradictory to us are not so in the light of heaven, and I take solace in the fact that it is not the preacher's responsibility to explain the unexplainable.

He also justified . . .

He declared us righteous on the basis of Christ's work. The great exchange of 2 Corinthians 5:21: our sins to Christ's account, his righteousness to ours. He bears the judgement that our sins deserve, in order to grant us the forgiveness that we do not deserve.

My primary school in Glasgow was such that we went to Greenbank Parish Church for our Christmas and Easter services. We would all go down there dutifully and take our place. I do not remember very much about those services except the very lovely church building and we sang hymns that have been etched into my memory: 'There is a green hill far away, outside a city wall; where the dear Lord was crucified, who died to save us all. I do not know, I cannot tell, what pains he had to bear; but we believe it was for us he hung and suffered there.' And I can remember even as a small boy, walking away from that and saying, 'In what sense was Jesus dying on the cross for us?' It has taken me a long time to figure it all out, for my understanding to catch up with my childhood expressions of faith, but it is this. Jesus did not die as a martyr, and he did not die as an example. He died as our substitute. What Paul is evincing here is what he has already worked out in the early chapters of chapter 8, so he can deal with justification in a moment as he passes.

He also glorified . . .

The interesting thing is that this verb is in the past tense, although the event is in the future. Why? Because in Christ it is a done deal. Let me finish in this way, because I think that this is the place where the emphasis ought to lie. The great task of the pastor and teacher is to persuade men and women of the greatness of God's love. Augustine said that the cross was the pulpit by which God preached his love to the world. When we come to verses like this, we need to remember that it is not the chain of salvation that saves, nor is it our understanding of the chain of salvation, nor is it our ability to articulate the chain of salvation. It is Jesus who saves. It is Jesus who has the supremacy when the sons and daughters of God are revealed in that great day and when that wonder of glorification takes place.

I am going to give the final quote to John Murray. This is what he writes in his *Writings Volume I*, page 59

> The passion for missions is quenched when we lose sight of the grandeur of the evangel. It is a fact that many, persuaded as they rightly are of the particularism of the plan of salvation and of its various corollaries, have found it difficult to proclaim the full, free and unrestricted overture of gospel grace. They have laboured under inhibitions arising from fear that in doing so they would impinge upon the sovereignty of God in his saving purposes and operations. The result is that though formerly assenting to the free offer of the gospel, they lack freedom in the presentation of the appeal and its demand.

It is because of the truth that is here in Romans 8:29 and 30 that we can go out into our communities and say to our loved ones, 'We implore you, on Christ's behalf, be reconciled to God. We want to tell you about a God who loves saving people. And if you have a minute I'd like to tell you how he saved me. Then I can also tell you how willing he is to do the same for you.'

Sometimes when we've done our best at trying to articulate that to people, we say to ourselves, 'I made such a mess of that. I hardly know what to say.' We bow down in prayer and then, in our prayers, we find we hardly know what to say. As we kneel down, and say 'Father' then the Spirit intercedes, taking our unspoken words and interpreting them before our Father. What a wonderful God!

Life in the Spirit 2: Romans 8:31

Introduction

I confess to a certain nostalgia when I think of Perry Mason. He was a fictional character created by a man by the name of Gardner. Gardner, I was staggered to discover, sold 150 million copies of his Perry Mason books. The character that he created was at the centre of what, in the fifties and sixties, was the longest running TV detective series. Perry Mason was a defence attorney and he was without question, week by week, always successful in defending his client. That is the reason I liked it. Righteousness always prevailed. His client had usually been put on trial for murder. The programme always built to the great closing argument, and we all sat on the edge of our seats to discover whether this would be the one week in which Perry Mason didn't manage to pull it off. Then we were able to breathe a sigh of relief and go to our beds contented because, as a result of his closing argument and putting all the evidence together, resolution had been available and freedom had been secured.

Basic and bold

I begin in that way because there is a sense in which this legally trained mind, this theologically constrained thinker, the apostle Paul, puts his closing argument together in verses 31 to 39. He does it in a masterful fashion. Unlike Perry Mason, he does not establish the innocence of his client – the client here being the believer in the Lord Jesus Christ. Perry Mason always said, 'My client is innocent because someone else is guilty.' That is not what Paul is doing. What he is doing is demonstrating that the believer is free from condemnation, not because he or she did not do it or was not guilty, because we *did* and we *are*. The believer is free from the condemnation that attaches to that guilt, however, because another, namely the Lord Jesus Christ, has borne the punishment in their place.

In Christ we have been given a new identity. In Christ we have adopted, or even been adopted, by a new mentality. We do not view things in the way that we once did, because we are in Christ. Also, in the Lord Jesus Christ, we have a new destiny.

It is this matter of God's completion of the work that he has begun that Paul addresses here at the end of Romans 8. In some ways, it is akin to what he says summarily in the sixth verse of Philippians chapter 1, where he reminds the Philippian believers that he is confident, and they should be too, that he who began a good work in them will bring it to completion in the day of Jesus Christ. And so what he is encouraging his readers to do is to think. There is about this closing argument a compelling logic. That is why he uses a formula that he has used prior to this: 'What, then, shall we say in response to this?' Paul is ending this glorious chapter on a high note, by asking some basic questions and by making a couple of bold declarations.

For and against

It is a reminder too of the orderly way in which he has progressed through this material. It is a reminder that our minds matter. It is a warning to us against adopting what we might refer to as a glandular Christianity. We know that the Bible encourages us to feel deeply about faith, but it also encourages us, demands of us, that we think deeply. He encourages us now to think along these lines with this series of questions.

The first one is in the second half of verse 31: 'If God is for us, who can be against us?' There is no uncertainty in this; the God who calls and the God who justifies is on our side. Therefore, with God on our side, whatever opposition comes our way, it is ultimately of no account. Paul is not suggesting that opposition does not exist. He does not ask the question, 'Who can be against us?' because the answer to that question is that many people can be against us. The evil one is against us, our conscience often is our accuser, and so on. He is asking the question: 'If God is for us, who can be against us?' He is saying that if we take all that is ranged against us and we set it against the fact of God's abiding presence on our behalf, then it puts all these things in perspective.

When you were at school, if you were a little chap, it was good to have a big friend. Sometimes you gave a bit of cheek to somebody and they said, 'I can take care of you.' Then you just stood aside. They looked at your big rugby-playing friend and said, 'Oh well, maybe not this afternoon.' It was not that no one was against you, it was that they realised that this chap made all the difference in the world. This is what the armies of Israel needed a lesson in. A lesson that came by way of a shepherd boy, who was not a notorious warrior. Nor was he someone clad as these mighty soldiers were clad, when every morning they marched out to hear the taunts of the great giant who was so clearly opposed to them that they forgot what they needed to be reminded of. It took David to show the giant what was of no account. 'If God be for us . . . you are nothing, Goliath.' That was the cry of God's people all the way through the Old Testament. 'If the Lord had not been on our side, what would have happened to us?'

Paul picks up that kind of Old Testament principle and reality, and he brings it home to the believers in his day. 'Let me prove it to you,' says Paul. 'If God is for us, who can be against us?' (v. 31). 'Here is the evidence,' he says. 'He did not spare his own Son.' When Jesus in the Garden prayed, 'If you are willing, take this cup from me,' the Father did not remove the cup of bitterness from Jesus, in order that those who are in Jesus might be able to drink the cup of blessing. Isaiah 53 says it was the will of God to crush him and to bruise him; he did not spare him, instead he gave him up for us as a substitute.

To think even for a moment of Christ as an unwilling participant in the Father's plan is nothing less than heresy. Earlier in the week, Stott's book, *The Cross* was recommended to us. Let me give you a quote from that same book. In fact it is a hybrid quote, but all that I am now about to say is Stott's, not mine

> When we talk of the Father's plan, and the Son's sacrifice, we should not think of the Father laying on the Son an ordeal he was unwilling to bear. Nor of the Son extracting from the Father a salvation he was unwilling to bestow. It is true that the Father gave the Son, it is equally true that the Son gave himself. We mustn't speak of God punishing Jesus, or of Jesus persuading God. We must never make Christ the object of God's punishment, or God the object of Christ's persuasion. For the Father and Son are subjects not objects, taking the initiative to save sinners.

If God be for us, then who actually can be against us? One plus God equals a majority.

The greatest and best

Secondly, 'How will he not also along with them graciously give us all things?' The logic is unassailable. If God has given us the greatest and the best in Jesus, he will not withhold all the gifts and blessings of grace that complete the work that his goodness has begun. In Christ all of the blessings are ours, and the story of our Christian experience is all that accompanies the wonder of our salvation in the Lord Jesus Christ. Paul again is asking us to think – do you think God would have given us his Son, sent him to the cross for us, and then be unwilling to give to us all the things that accompany his purposes?

Incidentally, 'give us all things' (v. 32) is a dangerous phrase if it is unearthed from the context. 'All things' does *not* mean that because God gave us salvation in Christ he will give us everything we want or everything we ask for, but all things that are necessary for the accomplishment of his purpose, 'to be conformed to the likeness of his Son' (v. 29).

Do you remember when you were hoping desperately for some toy at Christmas and as you removed the toy from the box, you saw 'Batteries not included'? So you had this thing which is a wonderful gift but you were on your own. That is not what God has done for us in Jesus. That is what Paul in part is saying here: 'He who did not spare his own Son but gave him up for us all in giving to us this wonderful gift, will he not along with him graciously give us all that is necessary for the completion of that which his goodness has begun?'

Case closed

Thirdly, verse 33: 'Who will bring any charge against those whom God has chosen?' Once again Paul is not suggesting that no charge may be brought. What he is saying is that any charge that is brought cannot stand, because the case is closed. The verdict has been rendered. Indeed, Romans 8 has begun with: 'Therefore, there is now no condemnation for those that are in Christ Jesus' – why? Because having been justified by faith, we have peace with God. Remember the great exchange – all of our demerits to Christ's account, and all of Christ's righteousness to our account. The righteousness that God requires of us, if we are ever to stand before him, is the righteousness that God reveals in the work of the gospel, the righteousness which Christ has achieved on our behalf, and the righteousness which God bestows upon all who believe.

So he says if people come to charge us with things, then who is really going to be able to do anything? And this is important, because Satan comes in our imaginations, into the court room, and he says to the Father, 'Look at that sinner. How can you declare them justified?' 'Well, yes,' says the Father, 'they are a sinner. The charges that you bring are valid, but will you look at my Son's hands? And look at my Son's feet? And will you look at the wounds in my Son's side? Who are you to condemn? It is Christ who justifies.'

This is the importance of understanding the atonement, of understanding the nature of what has happened in the cross, so that we are able to articulate it to ourselves and convey it to others. In the cross, God has satisfied his perfect and holy justice by executing the punishment our sins deserve. Without that, he would not be true to himself. And in the cross he pardons those who believe in Christ, even though they have sinned and deserve only condemnation. Without this, we as sinful men and women would be excluded from his presence for ever.

Now the way these verses fall and are translated in English is problematic. Verse 33: 'Who will bring any charge against those whom God has chosen? It is God who justifies.' There is a full stop in the NIV and verse 34 begins, 'Who is he that condemns? Christ Jesus who died' and so on. The way I try to read it is the way I try to understand it. It is God who justifies, who is he that condemns? If God has declared us without condemnation because of the work of his Son, who is going to bring any condemnation? The case is closed. Then I take it that what Paul does is simply state the facts, and the facts are in the balance of verse 34: 'Christ Jesus, who died' – the death of Jesus; 'more than that, who was raised to life' – the resurrected Jesus. We serve a risen Saviour. What possible good would a dead one be? It is as the risen Christ, it is as the living Lord, that Christ ensures the security of all who are in him. If salvation history has come to a crashing end in a Palestinian tomb, then we are actually involved in the greatest religious con trick that the world has ever seen.

'But,' says Paul, 'let me state the facts for you. The reason that I am able to say these things concerning no condemnation, and the reality of justification and the irrelevance of someone who comes to accuse you, is because we are dealing with Christ Jesus who died an atoning death, who was raised to life, who is at the right hand of God.' Where is Jesus? He is in the place of dominion and authority. What is he doing if he is physically present in heaven? We are told he is interceding for us. Not only does the Holy Spirit intercede concerning the groanings in our hearts, but Jesus intercedes on our behalf on the basis of his once-for-all work of atonement. He continues to secure for his people all the benefits of his death.

No separation

The fourth question that he asks is built on the prior three. Verse 35: 'Who shall separate us from the love of Christ?' Or 'What shall separate us from the love of Christ?' Then he lists enemies of our happiness and enemies of our potential security in Christ. Once again he returns to the sufferings that he had mentioned at the very beginning, the sufferings of this present time. Without a theology of suffering, we will fall prey to all kinds of temptation and we will find it far more difficult to speak to those who come to our churches suffering themselves.

Trouble, hardship, persecution, famine, nakedness, danger, sword – he lists them all and then he quotes the Bible. I wonder do you recognise where I am going, when I read these verses?

> 'I have been deprived of peace; I have forgotten what prosperity is. So I say, "My splendour is gone and all that I had hoped from the LORD." I remember my affliction and my wandering, the bitterness and the gall. I well remember them, and my soul is downcast within me. Yet this I call to mind and therefore I have hope: Because of the LORD's great love we are not consumed, for his compassions never fail. They are new every morning; great is your faithfulness. I say to myself, "The LORD is my portion; therefore I will wait for him"' (Lam. 3:17–24).

What Jeremiah is saying is this: 'Life is hard and God is good.' Paul reinforces it, as he comes in verse 37 to move to his great crescendo, which comes by way no longer now of questions, but in two great declarations.

Declaration one

'We are more than conquerors' (v. 37). *Hypernikomen*: sounds like a video game, doesn't it? He loads this word up: 'We are not just conquerors, we are more than conquerors. We are hyper-conquerors!' Now the reason he uses this word is because it is the only word that can do justice to the victory which is ours in the face of overwhelming odds. I am a hyper-conqueror in all these things – how can I be a conqueror in them? *In* them *through* him: notice prepositions are important. In all these things more than a conqueror, *through* him. Through him who did what? Who loved us. A love that has been demonstrated in the cross, a love that is a sustaining love, a love that is an everlasting love. It is not that he started to love us and then he stopped along the way, or his love is a diminishing love. His love knows no ends. There is no possibility of him baling out on us. Therefore, even though all hell lets loose against us, the accusations of conscience, the challenges of life, the immensity of the diminution of physical powers, the loss of personal relationships, the disintegration that comes by way of the ravages of sin; 'In all these things I am,' says Paul, 'more than a conqueror through him who continues to love us.'

Declaration two

The second great declaration is 'I am convinced' (v. 38). I like 'I am convinced'. In the King James Version it says, 'I am persuaded'. In the English Standard Version it is 'I am sure'. And it is a great encouragement when those to whom we look feel very confident about things. The early believers that are reading this letter, the initial believers in Rome, would be encouraged because for them tribulation and peril and the sword and famine were not things that you read about in missionary biographies. They were present realities. It would be a tremendous encouragement for them to say, 'The one who is writing this letter to us is also aware of these kind of sufferings, and what an encouragement it is to know that he is convinced, that he is sure.' 'I am persuaded' – how is he persuaded? He is persuaded by the facts. He is persuaded by the truthfulness of what he knows.

We can say a lot of things without knowing them. We can simply repeat them. But the Spirit of God teaches us first to know. And on the basis of what we know, then we say. And so what he is saying here is what he knows. 'I know' – this is not conjecture. 'I am absolutely convinced' – he is not working on the basis of his feelings; he is not flying in the turbulence looking out of the window, he is flying by using the instruments and the instruments are telling him what is true. If he looks out the window, it may only tyrannise him, it may only make him fearful, it may actually make him feel that he is flying upside down. It is vital that he flies with the instruments, and the same is true for you and me. We must fly by using the instruments. Let it be that which we know.

'I am sure,' he says, 'that nothing can and nothing will separate us from God's love.' Then he runs through all these things, potential or actual adversaries. 'Death nor life' – life with all its battles, potential triumphs or temptations, death like an ever-rolling stream. We are either one or the other. I am either going to be dead or I am going to be alive. Here's the good news: it does not matter if you are dead or alive, neither death nor life is going to separate you from God's love. 'Angels nor demons', the heavenly realms, whether they are of spiritual benefit or whether they are of spiritual wickedness, the unseen realms – through the cross, Jesus has disarmed all of those powers and authorities so 'neither angels nor demons, neither the present nor the future'. In other words, time is not going to be able to erode this either.

Time comes in at the rate of sixty seconds a minute. Augustine said, 'If you ask me what time is I know, but if you ask me to tell you, I do not know.' Time is mysterious. Time ages us. Time chases us. One of the benefits of age is wisdom. One of the hazards of age is worry. Neither the issues of time nor, he goes on, the issues of space will be able to impinge upon this. There is no chance. God is sovereign over both. And powers: 'nor any powers'. The forces of the Universe. 'Don't worry about them,' he says, 'nor anything else in all creation.' Nothing can, nothing will, 'separate us from the love of God that is in Christ Jesus our Lord' (v. 39).

Conclusion

We have gone full circle. There is no condemnation for those who are in Christ Jesus. Nothing can separate us from the love of God that is in Christ Jesus our Lord. In Jesus there is no condemnation, and there is no separation in Christ.

In my preparation for these studies I read a lot, and it got so bad that I just had to stop reading because I came upon a commentary on the first four verses of Romans 8 by Thomas Jacob that ran to about three hundred pages. It was a big book published by the Banner of Truth. It was vast and it was on only four verses. So that thoroughly depressed me, but I found a good quote on page seven and I said to myself, 'They will never know I didn't read the rest! In fact, they do not even know the book exists.' I had my secretary write this quote down for me. I said I want to use this as my conclusion to these studies, and so here it is. This is what Thomas Jacob writes in the preface to his studies on the first four verses of Romans 8

> If, in the discussing of these points, I have said nothing but what the learned in their treatises about them have said before, yet however two things I have done:
>
> According to my duty I have given my testimony to the great truths of God, let it signify what he pleases;
>
> I hope I have, I am sure it has been my endeavour, made some things, in themselves dark and intricate, to be somewhat more plain and intelligible to weaker capacities; and if I have done but that, though I have brought no new matter, my pains have not been ill-spent.
>
> My soul's desire is that the professors of this age may be well-grounded in the articles of the Christian faith, and that they may attain to a clearer insight into gospel mysteries than what as yet they have attained to; and if what is here done shall conduce to the promoting of these most desirable things, it will be a sufficient recompense to me for all the labour that I have been at.

Those sentiments are mine.

The Seminar

Personal renewal

by Amy and Frog Orr-Ewing

Amy and Frog Orr-Ewing

Amy Orr-Ewing is Training Director of RZIM Zacharias Trust and Director of Programmes for the Oxford Centre for Christian Apologetics, as well as a designate Trustee of Keswick Ministries. She is married to Frog [Francis] who is Vicar at All Saints Peckham.

Frog Orr-Ewing has been Vicar at All Saints Peckham since 2002. He became a Christian as a teenager, and studied theology at Oxford University and also had a year out working as a stockbroker. He is currently studying part-time for a PhD, and is an associate lecturer at St Mellitus College in London and a speaker for the Zacharias Trust.

Personal renewal: Haggai 1:1–6

Desperation

Throughout the Old Testament, there is a lot of talk about the presence of the Lord. When the presence of the Lord is talked about, there are two meanings: the first is the omnipresence of God, the existence of God, the inescapable reality of God. The second meaning is the manifest presence of the Lord. What is the opposite of being in God's presence? It cannot be absence because, as the psalmist says in Psalm 139:7, 'Where can I flee from your presence?' The opposite of presence is avoidance.

At the beginning of Haggai, we find the right response of the believer – a longing and desperation about our current state, and a reality about it. Why do we avoid God's presence? In my own life, when there has been struggle or unanswered prayer, desperation has not led to a greater intimacy with God but to an avoidance of God. For five years, we struggled to have children. I was praying about it every day, and it seemed as if everywhere I went, people were having babies. In our church in Peckham, we were seeing tremendous breakthroughs for salvation and healing, gang members becoming Christians through wonderful miraculous interventions, and yet we were in this terrible struggle ourselves.

The first step to personal renewal is desperation. To be desperate is good, if it brings us to our knees and to a place of honesty and intimacy with God. Let me encourage you, if there is an area of desperation in your own life, not to get up from the presence of God as Jonah did, and run away. One person said: 'I felt that if I began to cry, I would never be able to stop.' Here is a safe place, and to be desperate before the Lord is a good thing.

Frog: This passage in Haggai says, 'Give careful thought to your ways. You have planted much, but have harvested little.' There have been all these hopes and expectations, many of them have not been fulfilled, and what does the word of God say? 'It is time to build; it's time to rebuild; it is time to get the focus off your own panelled houses, your luxurious accommodation or whatever it might be, and to start thinking about God's house.' Obviously, as New Testament believers we realise that this is something we understand as the church, and in its original context it was the Temple in Jerusalem. We are a living temple, a living people. We are called to build God's church, across the world, but that is not to the exclusion of ourselves. As we think about this passage in the area of personal renewal, we realise that sometimes there is a rebuilding and building of our spiritual lives that needs to happen in us as individuals. We are going to look at reformation, reclamation and restoration as we look at Haggai 1, and what that might mean for us.

Reformation

Literally the word is re-formation, and as you look at Haggai, you are looking at this job of rebuilding a broken down Temple. It needs to be reformed. The original Reformation was not about saying, 'There has never been a church and we have got to build one from scratch!' It was an understanding that something had become broken down and twisted along the way, and we needed to reform and rework God's church. It is a constant process. Each generation needs to reflect on where we are at with Christ.

So the word of God comes to Haggai: 'Is it time for your panelled houses to be luxurious while God's house lies in ruins?' No. God's word says, 'It is time to rebuild.' It is reformation in the sense that there was already something there. They were not building on greenbelt land: this was a brownfield site. There was rubble, some of it was burnt, some destroyed and some half-standing. When Nehemiah goes around the walls of the city, broken down because of the same destructive forces a generation or so earlier, he needed to find his way over the rubble, in order to work out what the situation really was.

So, for personal renewal, you start with a sense of desperation, and then you begin to reflect on your own life. You realise there are elements of your spiritual life that are still standing, good things that God has made that are still in place, but that you need to work through the rubble. Spurgeon commented on Luther and Calvin, and on their preaching through the Reformation. He called Luther 'the master excavator' and said of Calvin that he 'laid bare long stretches of foundations of God's doctrine'. Good doctrine can separate out the rubble and the rubbish from the good stones. It is very important that we allow ourselves to come under good preaching, to help us work out what is rubbish and needs to be discarded, and what is of God and can be reused.

Preaching is not everybody's primary gift. Some church leaders are extraordinary community builders and pastors, but preaching is number ten on their skills list. So you need to ensure you have access to great preaching, to allow yourself this rubbish-sifting moment. Being Spurgeon fans, Amy and I love getting hold of volumes of sermons. When you are feeling tired and burnt out, the idea of sitting down for your quiet time and getting all the riches from God's word that you have heard that you must do seems difficult. In those times of exhaustion, open up a book of sermons. Allow yourself to be preached to by one of these great master excavators, who is good at separating the rubble from the rocks.

Reclamation and retrieval

Many stones, after you have separated them out from the rubbish, can be reused. A lot of St Peter's Basilica in Rome was built out of stones that were reclaimed from the Coliseum. If you look around older churches, you see stones and realise that they have lines in the wrong places. They have been reclaimed and put into the foundations of the next building. We can do the same. Andrew Walker has written brilliantly on this understanding of retrieval. He says this

> There is a wind of change blowing through the evangelical world carrying on its wings a new watchword which is neither renewal or revival but retrieval. The fact of its newness however should not deceive us into thinking that it is the title of yet another transitory technique of pragmatism born on the breezes of religious enthusiasm. Paradoxically what is new about retrieval is that it is a quest for something old and its modus operandi is not a technique but a turning back.

Not everything old is bad. In fact, many old things are good and are worth retrieving and reclaiming. There is great value in missionary biographies. We have found our personal renewal stirred again, as we read the stories of God's working with previous generations – the living stones. If you want to read an inspiring biography, how about Livingstone, the explorer? He went through the continent of Africa burdened by the sense that one day Africa was going to be filled with Christians, and they were going to go throughout the world sharing the gospel. During the course of his ministry, he led maybe only two people to Christ, and yet he had this driving sense that he had to open up the interior and go from country to country exploring, laying bare this extraordinary continent, so that others could come after him and start to preach the gospel. In London, the church decline stopped in about 1991 and has been in growth ever since. One of the major reasons for that, apart from the church planting that has been going on, has been the rise of African missionaries coming to London to reach the pagan West. David Livingstone poured himself out for this vision and this goal and, over one hundred years later, it has all become a reality.

If you want to read fantastic books, John Pollock has written countless biographies of great heroes of the faith, particularly from the nineteenth century. We would also recommend anything by or about

Hudson Taylor. There is an extraordinary two-volume book that has been published by Piquant. It is so helpful for us all to see what God has done with living stones in the past. Reclamation: find those living stones that have already been shaped, that have already been hewn out of the quarry and been put to use, and see if they can be of use to you as well.

Restoration and renewal

Haggai was told that the people needed to go up into the hills to bring back timber to rebuild. It is not enough just to clear away rubbish in our lives, to retrieve things of worth. We also need renewal and refreshment. The Temple needed new timber. 'Go up into the mountains and bring back timber and build the house [of the LORD]' (v. 8). What can I bring back that I have hewn and cut down in prayer, words from the Lord that I can take for the rest of the year and start building work?

New timber from the hills can be from Scripture. In your quiet time or daily Bible reading, pray first and then ask that God would speak to you and give you maybe one piece of fresh wood to build with, that day. You don't necessarily need five or six pieces of timber for each day, just one word of revelation, one thing that is from God direct to you, something that you know is from him.

I think we can also have an expectation of refreshment, an awakening that is a touch of the Holy Spirit within our lives. The book of Haggai is not just about a building, it is about wanting to meet with God face to face. That is the work of the Holy Spirit in the life of the believer. It is right for us to have that desperation and hunger. How do we know the full assurance of salvation? How do we know the Spirit within us cries, '*Abba*, Father'? This is a work of the Spirit, and if we are desperate for that felt, known sense of awakening and refreshment, God is pleased to meet with us by his Spirit. 'How much more,' says the Scriptures, 'will I give the Holy Spirit to those who ask for it? Just like a good father or even a bad father knows how to give good gifts to his children, how much more will I bring the Holy

Spirit?' Have your hearts open for that refreshment and awakening, that renewal of the Holy Spirit in your life.

Revival and salvation

Amy: Haggai 2:7 says, '"I will shake all nations, and the desired of all nations will come, and I will fill this house with glory," says the LORD Almighty.' What about renewal through evangelism? Sometimes I think we perceive renewal in our personal lives as something purely internal to us, something individualistic. But when the Holy Spirit is at work in us as believers, and when we are experiencing his renewal, it actually impacts our witness. Personal evangelism is an integral part of personal renewal.

A few years ago, we had a parents and toddlers group in our church. I was on maternity leave and so I was not preaching the gospel in the way that I was used to doing. I found myself with this group of other mums, and I was desperate to lead someone to Christ. Because I was the vicar's wife they ran away – they knew what was coming next! There was one girl in particular who had grown up in a Christian home. She had been a youth worker in a very prominent evangelical church but had fallen into sin, and had been disciplined by this church and excluded. She had completely turned away from Christ. She had been trained in personal evangelism too, so every starting opener sentence that I knew, she knew what was coming. So she would cut me off and say, 'I know where you are trying to go with this. You are trying to get me to identify with a sense of need for God and to admit that maybe I am in sin. Then you are going to introduce Jesus. Don't bother. I've rejected it. I've turned away. It's not going to happen. Don't talk to me any more about God. That's not why I come here. I come here so my children can play with the toys and I can meet other mums. I do not want to talk about God.'

Obviously I was really good as a personal evangelist – not! Anyway, a group of us carried on praying for her. Other women came to know Christ, and she resiliently held out. We had a few conversations, but it was hard. Then a few months later, I bumped into her in Sainsbury's. I had my two children in the trolley and she had her little boy in her trolley. I said, 'Hello. I have not seen you at the church group for the last few weeks.' She said, 'No.' Then suddenly God turned up. That is the only way I can describe it. She began to cry and I began to cry, and my babies began to cry and her baby began to cry. I could hardly speak, but I managed to say something about who the Lord is and that he was her Father and that it was time for her to come home. I led her in a very simple prayer and she became a Christian. It was wonderful and she is now a real stalwart member of our women's Bible study. She has gone through all sorts of extraordinary things and it is interesting hearing her perspective on the church discipline that she experienced, because she is thankful for it. She can see that she was in sin and she actually had to go through that period of being outside to recognise the seriousness of it.

Personal renewal in our lives will lead to fruit. If there are hard-hearted people in your life, keep going. My friend stands as a reminder to me that God loves to do the work of salvation, and renewal in our lives will lead to fruit. Perhaps there are children or grandchildren, parents or grandparents, long-standing friends in your life who have told you to back off, that they are never going to come to Christ. Personal renewal for us means that desperation, that breakthrough in personal evangelism.

This can sometimes take years. I was recently at a church in Oxford – Frog and I were at university there – and a girl came up to Frog. She is now working with a friend of ours from university, someone I have totally lost touch with. She had begun teaching and he is a teacher in the school she works in. She fell into conversation with him and mentioned that she was a Christian and that she goes to St Aldates, and invited him to come along. He said, 'What, St Aldates? I had these crazy friends at university called Frog and Amy. They were always inviting me to that church! I went to so many Christian Union evangelistic meetings with them. I never became a Christian, but I knew they desperately wanted me to, and they cared enough to invite me.' She said, 'Can I take over from them? Can I be your personal evangelist from today?' He said, 'Oh no!' There is someone who has not yet come through, but it was such an encouragement to me, how he perceived our evangelistic efforts. He was resistant, but to him it meant something. I am sure God is on his case.

Adoration and worship

The whole impetus of Haggai is about building the Temple, which was the place of worship and of adoration. Whether you are a good or a bad singer, engage in daily worship, not just daily Bible reading. Lots of books have been written about how worship is not just about singing and we know that. Worship is the whole of our lives, but worship is singing as well. Singing is incredibly important in the Bible. The psalms are full of it. The New Testament is full of it. What were Paul and Silas doing when they were in prison? They were singing, they were worshipping the Lord in that place of suffering. If you are married, do it together as a husband and wife. If you have children, sing and worship together as a family. It is amazing how it rubs off. Our little eighteen-month-old, Benjamin's favourite song is 'Happy Day'. It is incredible to see adoration of Christ even in our very small children, and the breakthrough that brings to our family life. There might be a situation that is very frustrating, and one of them might break into song. Even evangelistically, this has opened fantastic doors to share the gospel.

In our personal lives it is tremendously renewing to sing to the Lord, and if it sounds appalling, the Lord does not mind because he sees our hearts! The place of worship, and sung worship in particular, in the life of the individual as well as the corporate life of the church cannot be overplayed. Lest you think this is a female thing, men, let me encourage you with the experiences of Jim Elliot and his compatriots. They had a call from God to reach the Auca Indians. They were in their twenties, but knew that God had called them to go. They spent years preparing and they were martyred. The moments before their deaths, what were they doing? They had landed in a little aeroplane and they were standing together on the beach of the Amazon river singing a hymn.

Where in your life do you need courage? Where do you need to stand strong for Christ? Perhaps it is in a hostile family situation, where you know you are going to be mocked. Perhaps it is in the workplace. Remember those five strapping guys in their twenties, giving it all for Christ on a beach in the Amazon, about to die. Singing for them was not some namby-pamby experience – it was putting their faith into action. It was adoration and encouragement, all at the same time. That is why we need to sing. If Paul and Silas needed to sing in the stocks, we certainly needed to sing in Peckham when we faced death threats. Our telephone number was at the police station because someone was going to kill us, and he threatened to kill our children. He lived across the road, so he knew our comings and goings. He knew when I would be in the house on my own. When you face a situation like that, you need to be able to sing. Do not belittle the struggles of your own Christian life, whether it is the struggle to be a public Christian in the workplace, or in your community, or with your extended family. Be real that it is challenging to your courage, and sing in the face of that – give adoration to Christ.

Worship of Jesus and sung worship is integral to the renewed life of the believer. So if you do not have a hymn book at home, buy one. We collect old hymn books so we have Moody and Sankey and old Wesleyan hymn books as well as up-to-date songbooks too. Let singing and worship be part of your life.

Frog: When we moved into Peckham, I found something that I now like to call the archive. It was a metal box which I discovered, and in it were 120 copies of the Keswick hymn book from 1896. We got rid of eleven skip-loads of rubbish from within the church as we moved in and I decided it was time for a clearout. We were able to get hold of one of those hymn books, and it was great. I have no idea what any of the tunes are. You see these words and you sing them out, to whatever tune comes to mind. It is you and the Lord – and occasionally Amy banging on the ceiling from upstairs, particularly when I play my guitar. It is so encouraging to sing and to meditate or to speak out those hymns and songs.

Action

Amy: Part of Christian renewal and personal renewal is action. It is not all sitting around meditating and reading and having a quiet time. Action is involved too, and non-pious action. We can become weary with doing good, says the Bible, and that is a warning. Doing good and serving others, as well as resting, are choices that we make. See your areas of service as a part of your spiritual life – do not allow a dichotomy between the spiritual and the physical to build up. Writers such as Brother Lawrence and others are very profound on this subject. Those of you who have children will understand why my sister calls the first five years of raising a child 'the wiping years'. You are always wiping the table, wiping faces, wiping hands, wiping the floor, wiping the chair and then you cook again and then you are wiping again. For me, that process of washing up, drying up, putting things away, cooking food, wiping it off the floor again, is very boring. It is drudgery. But we can find Christ in those moments and think, 'I am serving my family today and, Jesus Christ, I am serving you.' Make prayer a part of our service, whether it is tidying up hymn books, or washing up the coffee cups at church, or running a youth club, whatever that area of service is.

Conviction

Not uncertainty! This is the word and the will of God. Haggai talks in these terms: 'The word of the Lord has come, the Lord declares this.' To be people who are shaped, and who are known as shaped, by the word of God, who are known to be people of conviction, is a truly counter-cultural thing today. It is something that we need Christ to do in us, because we are surrounded by a culture that tells us that we cannot be sure of anything, that there must be more than one way to heaven, that tolerance is king, and that to say we have found the truth would be arrogance in its fullness. That is not the worldview of the Bible at all. The worldview of the Bible is that God is there, that he has revealed himself in Christ, and that we can know him and we can know this is true.

We need conviction about who Christ is, and conviction about what his call on our life is as well. One of my favourite books is *Tortured for Christ*. I was given one of these five years ago at an event and if you have not, get it and read it. If you read it fifty or twenty years ago, read it again. It is mind-blowingly challenging. I want to read you just a quick excerpt as an illustration of what conviction looks like.

The book is about a couple called Sabina and Richard Wurmbrand. They are Romanian, they are pastors, Stalin has just taken over and is now in charge of their country. The communists have convened a congress of all the Christian bodies in the parliament building and pastor after pastor gets up and speaks words of praise about communism, assuring the new government of the loyalty of the church. Wurmbrand writes

> My wife and I were present at this congress. Sabina told me, 'Richard, stand up and wash away this shame from the face of Christ. They are spitting in his face.' I said to her, 'If I do so, you lose your husband.' She replied, 'I don't wish to have a coward as a husband.' And then I arose and I spoke to this congress, praising not the murderers of Christians, but Jesus Christ, stating that our loyalty is due first to him.

The consequences are that they are both imprisoned, and he describes the experience of his wife

> The mockery, the obscenity is horrible, the women were forced to work at hard labour building a canal, fulfilling the same workload as men, they shovelled earth in winter. Prostitutes were made overseers and competed in torturing the faithful. My wife has eaten grass like cattle to stay alive. Hungry prisoners ate rats and snakes. One of the joys of the guards on Sundays was to throw women into the Danube and then fish them out, to laugh at their wet bodies, to throw them back and fish them out again. My wife was thrown in the Danube in this manner.
>
> My son was left to wander on the street when his mother and father were taken away. Mihai had been very religious from childhood and

very interested in matters of faith. At the age of nine, when his parents
were taken away from him, he passed through a crisis in his Christian
life. He became bitter and questioned all of his religion. He had problems that children usually don't have at this age. He had to think about
earning his living.

It was a crime to help families of Christian martyrs. Two ladies who
helped him were arrested and beaten so badly that they were perma-
nently crippled. A lady who risked her life and took Mihai into her
house was sentenced to eight years in prison for the crime of having
helped families of prisoners. All of her teeth were kicked out and her
bones were broken. She will never be able to work again. She, too, will
be a cripple for life.

At the age of eleven, Mihai began to earn his living as a regular
worker. Suffering had produced a wavering in his faith. But after two
years of Sabina's imprisonment, he was allowed to see her. He went to
the communist prison and saw his mother behind iron bars. She was
dirty, thin, with calloused hands, wearing the shabby uniform of a pris-
oner. He scarcely recognised her. Her first words [Remember, she has
not seen her son for two years] were, 'Mihai, believe in Jesus!' The
guards, in a savage rage, pulled her away from Mihai and took her out.
Mihai wept seeing his mother dragged away. This minute was the
minute of his conversion. He knew that if Christ can be loved under
such circumstances, He surely is the true Saviour.

That is what conviction looks like. Lest we feel, 'I could never be like
that, I could never do that', we all feel that. Why are these books
written? They were written to inspire us. This is retrieval, Christians
who have gone before us. A part of that renewal of our spiritual life
is embracing conviction, allowing ourselves once again to be passionate about the truth, not to be overly concerned about how
others perceive us, and what the consequences might be to being
people of conviction and passion about the truth. Ask the Lord to
help you if that is an area where you waver. Ask him to give you that
conviction.

Cooperation

Frog: For personal renewal we are called to cooperation, and not isolation. It is said very often that Christianity is not a solo affair. Unless we are placed in solitary confinement like Richard Wurmbrand, following Christ means following Christ together. It means being part of the church, whether you like it or not. You belong to one another; as they say, you cannot pick your family. The same is true of the church. However, you can choose to work in cooperation with others, and I think it is important for us to realise that sometimes we need to be doing things side by side with people.

C.S. Lewis talks in his book *The Four Loves* about friendship. Friendship is what you do side by side as you are walking in the same direction, having a similar interest. You build up friendship and depth and warmth.

I have just touched base with a number of my old friends and we have been praying for and with one another. These are people I prayed with up to fourteen, fifteen, sixteen years ago. We were praying for each other to flourish and to move forward in ministry and follow Christ. Sixteen years later, many of us are married with children. Most of us are actually ordained. Now in our mid to late thirties, almost all of my friendship group are leading churches across the country at the moment. We were renewing our faith, renewing one another in prayer, laying hands on each other, crying out to God for more of the Holy Spirit and more conviction, and for God's provision in the steps of faith we were taking. We all needed to see God provide for our families. Friendship is so important.

In our personal renewal, when we are feeling slightly weary, that is when we need our friends. Very seldom do all of us hit a rocky patch at the same time. Rather than looking around at our friends and feeling that they are smug and that they have got it all together, we should work in cooperation – whether that be in a family, as a couple, or with our children. Often we ask our children to pray for us if one of us is sick, or we are going to go out to preach. We say, 'We're a mission team.' In January, we were going through South Carolina and Washington. We were speaking in Annapolis, the naval academy there, doing all sorts of things, and our children were saying, 'We are a mission team. We are team members.' It was important, that sense of shared cooperation. They realised then that it was not just a question of Mummy and Daddy going away. This was a mission team. That was their part to play – to pray as we went and did these things.

Sometimes we need to be in a team. Find yourself in an environment with two or three others, minimum, where you can be encouraging, comforting and strengthening. That may well be your small group or your home group, but often it is not. You want to be with people who encourage you. My father says the best way to improve your tennis game is to play tennis with somebody better than you. Spend time with people who inspire you. There may be something about your life which inspires them, but do not worry about that. Find people, whom you like spending time with, who draw out the best of Christ in you.

In Peckham, we have had a largeish team the last seven years – up to twenty-four people on the ministry team in the church. It is really interesting seeing people as they leave that team and go solo for a bit, just watching some of that passion slightly dampen down. They were so much more in a team than they were on their own, and that is true of me. We need to be in teams.

Vocation and commission

In Haggai, the Spirit of God stirred up the whole people to work together. God's Spirit stirs up a whole people, so allow the Spirit of God to do that in the area that you are called to. Also in this Haggai passage, Zerubbabel, Joshua (or Jeshua) and Haggai are key leaders. They have a sense of vocation and calling. One of them is a high priest, one of them is a governor, one of them is a prophet, and each one of them has to fulfil their task. They find who they are in Christ by doing what they are truly called to do.

That is one of the true liberating elements of being the body of Christ and each of us serving a different purpose – we find our fulfilment and our renewal to the extent that we are operating in our areas of primary calling, where we know that we are doing what God called us to do. It may be totally quirky, totally individual, or it may be something very similar to somebody else. We do not discover personal renewal by trying to copy somebody else's ministry or calling, or to copy a pattern of life that we see somebody else having. If you are single, looking at married couples with their children and longing for that, you may feel you are not going to come in to spiritual renewal until you have that pattern of life. Or vice versa, you may be exhausted from getting up at five in the morning for four years in a row and longing for carefree days when you do not have to do that any more. You may think, 'If only I had more time on my hands and I was not so exhausted, then I would be in a place of personal renewal!' Or perhaps you are thinking, 'If only I was not heading into retirement and the twilight years and I had all of my energy again, then I could be effective for Christ.'

What are you called to do? That is something your relationship with God can really tell you about!

The Addresses

Springs without water

by Derek Burnside

Derek Burnside

Derek Burnside is a Trustee of Keswick Ministries and on the staff and Leadership Team at Belmont Chapel in Exeter. He also teaches at four of Torchbearer's European Bible Schools and is on the Councils of the EA and Partnership UK, the network of British churches from Brethren backgrounds. Previously he taught RE and was a UCCF staff worker. Derek is married to Penny. When not doing any of the above he is most likely to be found reading a book, watching a film or riding a bike.

Springs without water: 2 Peter 2

Introduction

My parents were both smokers. They were thoughtful and careful and slightly guilty smokers, always doing their best to avoid inflicting their fug on me or my sister, but seeing our parents puffing away was part of our upbringing. According to some studies, that gave me an above average chance of taking up the habit myself. I never did.

Why not? There were lots of reasons. I loved sport, and knew smoking wouldn't help me run any faster. I hated the smell. As a teenager, any residual glamour or rebellion in a cigarette soon drifted away when it was something you saw your mum and dad do every day. Discovering later in my teens that my body was a gift from God and his dwelling place was certainly a factor. But none of these was the clincher. I'd made the firm decision never to smoke when I was nine, and I remember the moment – and the real reason – to this day. One afternoon in primary school, sitting in grey flannel shorts on a polished parquet floor, we were shown a flickery reel-to-reel health education film about the dangers of smoking. On screen was a cancer patient lunging for air through a hole in his throat. With wheezy, cracked breaths he pleaded with his young hearers never to make the same mistake he had made; don't smoke. I listened, and made my decision that afternoon.

Sometimes the most loving thing we can do for another person is warn them. Sometimes, the most positive thing we can do is be negative. That is worth remembering as we read a passage as apparently gloomy as 2 Peter 2, with all its talk of heresies, exploitation and destruction, a passage that might seem incongruous as the focus for an evening 'celebration'. Yet we should be celebrating the fact that we have a heavenly Father who loves us enough to warn us, and who is positive enough to be negative.

The last time I was urgently thirsty was on a push bike in summer Pyrenees heat. With a friend I'd entered a French race that took us over three mountain passes in one day. As I neared the summit of the second hill, I was in serious need of the promised 'water station' at the top, a truck with its tailgate down and bottles being handed off the back to the dehydrated cyclists slogging past. There had been, however, a serious miscalculation by the race organisers on that sweltering day. The first few hundred cyclists through had drunk the van dry: there was no water left. Along with about a third of the field, I failed to finish the race.

For travellers in dry lands (like the one the first readers of this letter lived in) springs without water (2:17) are bitter, serious and potentially life-threatening disappointments. They will promise everything but deliver nothing, and in the process will damage – and even destroy – those who place their trust in them. To warn someone that dry, killing emptiness is masquerading as life-bringing nourishment is an act of the greatest love.

Previously in 2 Peter . . .

These evenings in 2 Peter are titled 'An urgent call for Christian growth.' Let's remind ourselves what we've heard so far.

On Saturday Jonathan Lamb reminded us that 'Christ is enough!' 'Your faith is as precious as ours,' (1:1) Peter the apostle tells his hearers. Why? 'Because His divine power has given us everything we need for life and godliness through our knowledge of him' (1:3). Peter's first urgent call to Christian growth is to remember that, in Christ, we have everything.

On Sunday Hugh Palmer urged us to 'Be eager to make your calling and election sure' (1:10). The life truly given by Christ and empowered by Christ will result in Christ-centred renewal. It will bear the likeness of Jesus and will be effective and productive; 'add to your faith goodness, knowledge, self-control, perseverance godliness, brotherly kindness, love' (1:5).

Then last night Jonathan Stephen showed us the precious, prophetic God-promise foreshadowed at the transfiguration that so obsesses Peter as he calls us urgently to growth in Christ: Jesus Christ is coming back.

Peter's urgent call

So, what is Peter's urgent call to Christian growth for us tonight? Just before we look at it, flick back what is probably just a page in your Bible, to 1 Peter 5:8–9: 'Be self-controlled and alert. Your enemy the devil prowls around like a roaring lion, looking for someone to devour. Resist him, standing firm in the faith, because you know that your brothers throughout the world are undergoing the same kinds of sufferings.'

2 Peter 2 describes one way in which our enemy 'prowls to devour' – through false teachers. Peter's urgent call to Christian growth tonight is this: be alert to the presence of false teachers in the church. He assures his readers that 'there will be false teachers among you' (2:1). There will be 'springs without water' (2:17), promising everything but delivering nothing, damaging and even destroying those who trust in their empty words, threatening our capacity to finish the race we have started. Rely on them at your peril.

Before we go any further, let's ask ourselves a question; why is false teaching so dangerous? Why does Scripture warn us so vividly against it? Because truth matters: the way we live our lives is determined by what we believe about ultimate realities. So if we believe things that aren't true, we live badly.

In some areas, of course, it doesn't matter all that much if we get ultimate reality wrong. Let's imagine that this is your first time in Keswick, and that a friend told you before you came that the town has an annual average rainfall of only three days a year, and that it never rains in July. Let's imagine that you believed them and packed accordingly. Basing your life on that piece of false teaching will have inconvenienced you only mildly, until you managed to get out and buy yourself a mac and a brolly.

But let's imagine that you believe something untrue about ultimate reality that really does matter. Like, for example, the existence of an all-powerful, reigning, perfect, glorious God, and your helpless state of rebellion towards him. Or your enslavement to sin, and his real and coming judgement on it. Or his immeasurable love for you, and the fact that the only way of escaping his judgement is through having your sin atoned for at Christ's cross. Get any of those ultimate realities wrong and the consequences will be disastrous. That really will matter. Believe 'made up stories' (2:3) rather than God-revealed truth and that will certainly affect the way you live now, and it may affect your eternal destiny.

That is why false teaching matters so very, very much. Tonight's urgent call to Christian growth is to be alert to the presence of false teachers in the church; 'There will be false teachers among you' (2:1). John Calvin's response to this verse is sobering and helpful; 'The Spirit of God has declared once and for all that the church will never be free from this internal trouble.'

Where are these false teachers?

Many of us will be here this week not just for the teaching, but also for the setting. Lots of you in this tent will be walkers. You will know that moment when you are high on a hill and can see a succession of ridges stretching before you: multiple mini-horizons. As we think about where false teaching might be found, let's briefly scan four horizons.

Contemporary culture

The first horizon is the wider world outside the church. Although this is not Peter's main concern in this chapter, we would be foolish to forget that living in this world, for all its joys, also involves standing in the chilly drizzle of constant false teaching. The biggest contemporary heresy of all may be that there are no heresies; to believe in them demands a belief in absolute truth, and many of us here are rooted in societies that increasingly talk about values we construct, not ultimate truths that God reveals.

Another contemporary heresy is an increasingly aggressive atheism. Don Carson describes vividly the way those sorts of false teachings can build over time: 'An atheistic framework is never established by a single individual. It is built up piece by piece until certain beliefs are culturally possible, then probable, then almost inevitable – and each generation, each individual, has contributed to this massive rebellion, this lust for autonomy that refuses to recognise the rights of our Maker and our obligations to him.'[1] In the West, we are currently living in the midst of just such a 'massive rebellion'. To live and engage with our wider world will inevitably involve frequent encounters with false teachings.

The global church

The easiest and 'safest' false teachers to spot are often the ones on the other side of an ocean. As we read in 2 Peter 2 of destructive heresies, boastful arrogance, sexual immorality and a greed for money, we might be remembering tragic stories we've read of distant power-crazed pastors who exploit their congregations, of disgraced televangelists, of prominent ministries felled by sexual sin, or of distant sub-Christian cults where a patina of biblical language can't conceal that this 'church' has precious little to do with the Lord Jesus Christ.

Closer to home?

The tougher, less comfortable ridge to scan will be our own denomination, possibly even our own congregation. As we read Peter's descriptions of waterless springs, and hear about the variants on true doctrine that were leading people away from saving faith in Christ and into immorality, we must be alert to the possibility that these sorts

---

[1] D.A. Carson, *For the Love of God, volume 2* (Wheaton: Crossway books, 1999). Notes for August 11th (pages unnumbered).

of ideas and influences are in our own churches. The 'feast' Peter talks about in verse 13 is probably referring to the meal at which the death of Christ was remembered, the equivalent of our modern-day communion services. That's certainly the meaning in the parallel passage in Jude verse 12, from which Peter appears to draw. These false teachers were embedded in the local church.

In the 'Church and Community Renewal' seminar stream at the Convention this morning, Hugh Palmer was talking on 'Renewing our Teaching.' He had spoken eloquently on searching the Scriptures, praying for spiritual understanding, wanting to please God and not people, and being doers of the word and not just hearers. During the Question and Answer session, there was this question: 'What do you do when a quarter of your church – an evangelical church – don't believe a word you've just said?' When we do find false teachers in our own congregations, Peter tells us, we should not be surprised.

Our own minds and hearts

This horizon is the closest and toughest horizon of all to scan. Peter is clear that his readers will be exploited by these teachers; 'Many will follow their shameful ways' (2:2). These heresies are persuasive and seductive, so we must have the courage to ask ourselves some tough questions. Have we been influenced by these ideas? Are we tempted by these persuasive lies? May we even have played a part in spreading them? Have you or I been a dry and bitter disappointment to the spiritually thirsty, because we have wandered away from God's word, given too much attention to made up stories and been unable to offer people Jesus?

How should we respond to false teachers?

As we explore what could be a worrying theme, let's remember again how Peter trains us to fight off spiritual attack. Waking up to the reality that false teaching is alive and well and possibly coming to a church near you could easily flip us into a spin of panic and paranoia. We can do better, Peter says.

Let's be 'self-controlled' (1 Pet. 5:8), not panicky. There will be no wild-eyed, flailing accusations, no over-zealous witch hunts. We will resist the temptation to flounce home and denounce the deacons or exorcise the elders. 2 Peter 2:10 and 11 are not easy verses to understand, but a popular reading is that the false teachers were slandering the fallen angels referred to back in verse 4, possibly the figures we read about in Genesis 6. Even though those angels had sinned, throwing slanderous accusations around against them was a place where even faithful angels feared to tread. So we are not going to imitate the very false teachers we oppose by arrogantly, carelessly and ignorantly throwing around slanderous allegations, even when there may be wrongdoing to challenge. We will remember Jesus' parable of the wheat and the weeds; it will be the angels' job 'to weed out of his kingdom everything that causes sin and all who do evil' (Matt. 13:41). When faced with false teaching, we will be self-controlled.

Peter also calls us, though, to be 'alert' to this danger, neither complacent nor naïve, and to 'resist, standing firm' knowing that we are not unique or alone in facing this struggle (1 Pet. 5:8–9). We will be greatly encouraged and strengthened knowing that 'the Lord knows how to rescue the godly from trials.' Yes, false teachers will be in the church's midst, but if God 'protected Noah' and if God 'rescued Lot' he will of course do the same for us (2 Pet. 2: 5–9).

So: tonight's urgent call to Christ-centred renewal? Be alert to the presence of false teachers in the church.

What do these false teachers look like?

My favourite read as a small boy was *The Observer's Book of Aircraft*, a pocket book that gave silhouette outlines of different aircraft. Not every detail was included, just enough to get the shape into your head so you could recognise a plane when you saw it. 2 Peter 2 is part of the Bible's *Observer's Book of False Teachers*. We know they will be in the world and in the church, but what do they look like? Can we get to know their rough outline, so we'll know one when we see one?

'Be free!'

'They promise them freedom' (2:19). 'Freedom!' is the false teachers' catchphrase. In itself, of course, freedom is admirable and just what

Jesus promised for those who truly follow him (John 8:36). But it is a twisted sort of 'freedom' that these false teachers offer. Let's look at what they 'free' their followers from.

'Be free from Christ's rule'

The 'freedom' on offer involves 'even denying the sovereign Lord who bought them' (2:1). The words translated 'sovereign Lord' and 'bought' are both straight from the marketplace and refer to a slave owner – one who possesses another because he has purchased him. The first identifying feature of a false teacher will be to deny God's right of ownership over human lives.

Let's just press the 'pause' button for a moment, because there's an intriguing question in verse 1; what exactly does Peter mean by the phrases 'sovereign Lord' and 'bought'? If 'sovereign Lord' means 'Jesus', and 'bought' means 'redeemed' or 'saved', that has huge consequences. Peter would be implying that a saving faith can be lost – and these men are certainly lost: look at the way verse 1 ends – 'they are bringing swift destruction on themselves.'

Wayne Grudem makes an alternative suggestion;[2] this may not be a reference to the cross at all. Maybe, Grudem thinks, Peter is quoting Moses in Deuteronomy 32 as he slams into rebellious Israelites: 'Is this the way you repay the LORD, O foolish and unwise people? Is he not your Father, your Creator, who made you and formed you?' (Deut. 32:6). By that reading, these false teachers are being rebuked for repeating the mistakes of their rebellious Jewish ancestors. God had brought them out of Egypt, but they were ungrateful and disobedient. On that reading, these false teachers deny the same Lord who bought the Israelites out of slavery in Egypt; it is not necessarily a statement that they had ever truly been bought with the blood of Christ.

What is certain is that these teachers do not put themselves under Christ's authority – his ownership. They do not believe that they are his, or that he has bought them with his blood. Before we explore their teachings or their behaviour or their impact, let's imprint this

---

[2] Wayne Grudem, *Systematic Theology* (Leicester: IVP, 1994), p.615.

defining silhouette on our minds. This is their essential failing, their key characteristic: they deny that they are Christ's. They cry 'freedom' from Jesus himself. They 'despise authority' (2:10), and Christ's authority in particular. These are men and women who simply deny that they are slaves of Jesus, and lure others to the same spurious 'freedom'.

'Be free from Christ's return'
Surely it is a highly dangerous move to declare yourself independent from a powerful king who is going to come and condemn you for your rebellion? The false teachers' strategy is simply to free themselves from Jesus' coming judgement by denying it will happen; 'They will say, "Where is this 'coming' he promised? Ever since our fathers died, everything goes on as it has since the beginning of creation"' (3:4). They teach that Jesus is not coming back. If they are free from Christ's return, they are free from God's judgement. When Peter says that 'their destruction has not been sleeping' (2:3), he may be turning one of their own phrases back on themselves. Is that what the false teachers have been saying about God? 'Where is Jesus, then, if he's coming back? God and his coming judgement must be asleep!' Have they really been foolish enough to taunt heaven in the same sort of way that Elijah taunted the prophets of Baal (1 Kings 18:27)? They will soon discover just how alert and watchful the living God actually is.

'Be free to indulge your every desire'
A few moments ago we reminded ourselves just why false teaching is so dangerous: get essential facts about ultimate reality wrong, and we begin to make major mistakes in the way we live. Peter now shows us how the impact of wrong beliefs starts to corrode the quality of everyday life. Now that these teachers have 'freed' themselves from Christ's rule, Christ's return and Christ's judgement, they are of course free to do whatever they want. After all, who's going to hold them to account now? So they indulge their physical desires, however damaging that might prove to themselves, or to others, or to the church itself. 'Their idea of pleasure is to carouse in broad daylight' (2:13); they are drunk in the middle of the day, shameful behaviour in the ancient world even by pagan standards. They have 'eyes full of adultery' (2:14),

literally 'eyes full of an adulteress'; they are so sex-driven that they cannot look on another person without thinking about 'having' them.

Are we getting the shape of these false teachers? Will we know one when we see one? 'If you free yourself from an impending encounter with the returning, judging Jesus Christ, you free yourself to do whatever you want. Tell yourself that you are not his, you are not bought, he is not boss and he is not coming back, and you have set yourself free to do whatever you want.'

Aspects of that sort of teaching are all around us. Here is Julian Baggini, editor of *The Philosophers' Magazine*, writing in *The Times* just a few days ago about a scene in the film Toy Story 3 in which Woody, Buzz and their friends are nearly incinerated, but just get rescued in time.

> With its inventiveness and wit, *Toy Story* has been hailed as a grown up immaturity, that says that humankind cannot deal with the absence of a higher authority and the freedom and responsibility that comes with it. Camus wrote, 'without a master, the weight of days is dreadful'. *Toy Story 3* peers over the precipice of mortality only to step back to the consolations of religion.

Grow up, Baggini calls. There is no higher authority. Stop hiding in the immature consolation of believing in God, admit he's absent, and have the courage to be 'free'.

The inside story

There was another kind of aeroplane drawing I loved as a child, called a 'cutaway', where the artist showed what was happening on the inside of the aircraft, beneath its metal skin. Peter does a similar thing; as well as outlining the defining lines of these first-century false teachers, he gives us a glimpse of what is going on beneath the surface appearances.

Enslaved

Although they 'despise authority' these false teachers are anything but free. They are followers too, but instead of following Jesus they follow the 'corrupt desire of the sinful nature' (2:10). They might promise freedom, but they can't even free themselves: 'they themselves are slaves of depravity – for a man is a slave to whatever has mastered him' (2:19). They are in the grip of their impulses, powerless to resist, 'like brute beasts, creatures of instinct' (2:12). Their appetites for alcohol, sex and money have enslaved them. Like Balaam, they are trying to harm God's people for cash (2:15–16).

Condemned

The future for these false teachers is desperate. 'Their condemnation has long been hanging over them, and their destruction has not been sleeping' (2:3). Little wonder that things are this serious for them when we consider the havoc their lies have brought. Peter pictures their followers as fish caught on hooks: 'by appealing to the lustful desires of sinful human nature, they entice people who are just escaping from those who live in error' (2:18). These teachers have dangled the poisonous bait of consequence-free indulgence, and many have bitten. Particularly vulnerable were those just becoming spiritually awakened, who now find themselves hooked by a false gospel. The reputation of the church has been seriously damaged in the process; the community of God's people that should be travelling towards radiance, holiness and purity is now stained by these 'blots and blemishes' (2:13).

Peter asks the blunt question: what possible grounds do these people have for thinking that God will not judge such an attack on his people and his purposes? His track record of judging and punishing the rebellious and the disobedient is clear. The false teachers can make up all the stories they want, but towering above them all is the biblical witness that rebellious angels, the ungodly of Noah's day and the lawless of Sodom and Gomorrah are judged and punished and await the ultimate reckoning on the 'day of judgement' (2:9).

Hugh Palmer reminded us on Sunday what it looks like to make 'your calling and election sure' (2 Pet. 1:10). This chapter gives a vivid example of what not doing so looks like. These teachers gave every appearance of knowing Jesus and escaping the corruption of the world; they heard the gospel and seemed to accept it. But they made no progress, and then turned their backs on it. And as if that was not bad enough, they then created their own awful version of 'good news' which simply pandered to the destructive instincts of the old sinful nature. Gift-wrapping it in glittery paper marked 'freedom', they hawked their vicious junk around the church itself.

With two brutal proverbs Peter sums them up (2:22); they have been sick, but rather than walk away, they return to their vomit and eat it. They have had the chance of being cleansed by Christ, but instead they are washing in mud and calling others over to join them.

What should we do?

2 Peter 2 is a call to us all to be alert to the continuing danger of false teaching within the church. Whether the horizon is near or far, God's people must stay vigilant and, without panic or surprise, firmly resist the influence of voices that preach a false gospel.

As we examine ourselves tonight, let's not forget that the one who penned these words knew what it felt like to deny Jesus. We should be clear that the spasms of idleness or fear that are common to all of us are not what Peter condemns in this chapter; his focus in on a deliberate, aware, settled opposition to Christ. But nevertheless, part of Peter's purpose is to warn us. Do we see any shadows of the false teachers' distinctives creeping over our own lives? Are we prone to their casual shrugging-off of Christ's Lordship? Do our church programmes and evangelism downplay the Second Coming, effectively dismissing the reality of God's coming judgement? Are we increasingly snapping the cords of the sinful nature we've been freed from: the love of money, the tyranny of lust, the exploitation of others, the centrality of self? Or are we ever tempted to sniff around our own old vomit, or make the occasional mud pie?

Where is the world heading?

by Jonathan Stephen

Jonathan Stephen

Jonathan Stephen became a Christian while studying sociology at university in Bangor, North Wales. He was in pastoral ministry for nearly 28 years before becoming Principal of WEST in 2006. Jonathan has served the wider church through his preaching ministry and involvement in many Christian projects and agencies. Past President of the FIEC and present Director of Affinity, Jonathan is deeply grateful to God for his wife, Sheila, and their son, Jeremy. Jonathan is an avid sports fan and, as a member of MCC, takes his guardianship of the laws of cricket very seriously!

Where is the world heading?
2 Peter 3:1–13

I have to admit I am a sucker for those popular science books that promise to unravel the mysteries of the Universe. It is been said that there is speculation, then there is wild speculation, and then there is cosmology! There are plenty of people who write about the origins and nature of the Universe who perhaps do not have a lot of evidence for what they say. I can tell you what parallel universes are and wax lyrical on superstring theory – because, quite frankly, nobody can contradict you, so you are perfectly safe on all of these things. The trouble is, with most of these theories, they suffer from a fatal flaw: the assumption of a closed system. Somehow, the space-time continuum had to bring itself about. In virtually all these theories, advanced by extremely clever people sometimes, there is no room for anything outside. To put in bluntly, there is no room for any God in the construction of the Universe.

2 Peter 3 is one of the most extraordinary chapters in the Bible because it introduces us to the only cosmology that ultimately matters: the cosmology of the one who created, sustains and will ultimately transform this Universe – the cosmology of God. It tells us how our present Universe began and how it is going to end. Long before any physicist guessed the connection, the apostle shifts easily, in this passage, between space and time – both of which are vital themes for an understanding of it. Long before Albert Einstein proposed his

theories, Peter knew that time is relative. It can be viewed from outside, from eternity, very differently. Verse 8: 'do not forget this one
thing, dear friends: With the Lord a day is like a thousand years, and a
thousand years are like a day.' Time can be slowed down by a patient
Creator (v. 9) or, even more remarkably, time can be speeded up by
godly believers (v. 12). Time is flexible. What an amazing Universe we
inhabit.

Having said all that, this chapter is not a scientific treatise. It is an
urgent and passionate plea to believers and unbelievers alike to prepare for the day of the Lord, when the Son of God will come back
and manifest himself in power and glory in order to judge all humanity, to purge the creation of evil and its consequences once and for all,
and to establish his eternal, merciful and loving rule over a brilliantly
renewed heaven and earth. So let's look at it together.

New creation

In 2 Peter 3:1,2 we read: 'Dear friends, this is now my second letter to
you' – that is a pretty insipid translation in the NIV. I love the NIV but
the word is 'beloved' and it is important for us to realise that Peter
cares passionately for these people he is writing to. It makes a great
difference in the way he speaks to them and, indeed, what he says to
them: 'Beloved, this is now my second letter to you. I have written
both of them as reminders to stimulate you to wholesome thinking. I
want you to recall the words spoken to you in the past by the holy
prophets of the Old Testament and the command given by our Lord
and Saviour, through your apostles' of whom he was one, in what we
regard as the New Testament. We need to use our renewed minds to
get around the shared central themes of both the Old Testament
prophets and the New Testament apostles, and to realise that the Bible
tells us all we need to know about these vital truths about God's creation, humankind's fall and Christ's redemption.

The Bible tells us, through a living faith, we have to join the
vanguard of this coming new creation. I always loved the thought that
we are new creatures in Christ; we are the beginning; we are new

creatures living in an old creation. The old creation that we live in is passing away. What seems real to the unbeliever is going to be burnt up, as it were, in the general fire, but we are going to go on – we are the advanced guard of the new creation. Peter wants us to understand these things for ourselves. Says Peter, 'I want you to recall these things – even if, at this time, you forget everything else. Whatever the false prophets teach, fix your eyes on the day of the Lord and on his return, and live in the light of it.'

That is quite amazing, because the Scripture often tells us to remember things that we think we'd never forget. The Scripture says, 'Remember Jesus Christ' – how on earth are we going to forget Jesus Christ if we are reading the New Testament? And yet, it is almost as incredible when Peter says, 'Remember the day of the Lord.' Heaven knows, it would be hard enough for anyone to forget the great climax of history – which virtually the whole Bible refers to – which lies ahead for all of us. It is trumpeted throughout the Scriptures, both the Old and the New Testaments; it is so clear, and yet we are told to recall these things. And, of course, we need to remember because it remains a terrible, general failing of fallen human beings to forget these things and put them out of our minds.

In order that we might remember, Peter tells us in this passage about two kinds of forgetfulness. First of all, he talks about the fatal forgetfulness of the godless (vs. 3–7) and then he speaks about the more innocent but nonetheless dangerous forgetfulness of the godly (vs. 8–10).

Forgetfulness of the godless

Verses 3–7

> First of all, you must understand that in the last days scoffers will come, scoffing and following their own evil desires. They will say, 'Where is this "coming" he promised? Ever since our fathers died, everything goes on as it has since the beginning of creation.' But they deliberately forget that long ago by God's word the heavens existed and the

earth was formed out of water and by water. By these waters also the world of that time was deluged and destroyed. By the same word the present heavens and earth are reserved for fire, being kept for the Day of Judgment and destruction of ungodly men.

Peter talks about the 'last days' in verse 3; the 'last days' do not mean the very last few days of the week before the Lord Jesus Christ returns but they refer, as always in the New Testament, to the whole period between Christ's first and second comings.

Put yourself back in Peter's day and imagine yourself amongst this generation. It did not take more than a few years after the ascension of the Lord Jesus back into heaven for people to start deriding Christ's promise to return. Scoffers rose up very quickly. Very soon, just a few years after these things, people were saying, 'It is taking an awfully long time, isn't it? Is he really coming back? Did he really mean it or did he mean something else? We have imagined he is going to literally come back and it is going to be a great dramatic event, but maybe we have got it wrong. Maybe it was just a spiritual thing. Maybe it has even happened already.' False teachers would come in and play upon that.

Throughout this letter, Peter has stressed the obvious link between denying the day of judgement, in all its literal reality, and 'following evil desires'. 'If we do not have the day of judgment in front of us,' he says, 'evil men will get worse.' And, of course, there is no incentive to live a holy life. There is no judgement, God does not mind, God is not going to intervene, nothing supernatural is going to take place. Apparently, these 'scoffers' backed up their claim by saying God had never intervened supernaturally since the earliest humans had walked the earth. 'God does not operate in that way' – that is what they would say. 'There is no evidence that he ever has operated in that way.' God is not going to come dramatically and Jesus is not going to return in this way.

It does sound remarkably like modern atheistic evolutionists, with their views that nothing dramatic or miraculous has happened. 'It just takes a long time, doesn't it, for everything to form?' – and the earth is four billion years old, by the latest reckoning – 'It takes time and we just have to ask ourselves the question: How many millions of years does it take to produce *homo sapiens* upon the earth? All of these questions are open because there is no dramatic input, nothing dramatic happens, it is a slow uniform process.' That is the classic view of evolution and God has no part in it. In a sense, what we hear today is not new at all. There were people back in Bible times and, no doubt, hundreds if not thousands of years before, who had exactly the same godless view of how things were. So we should not be shaken by these things; they come in slightly different forms but that was certainly the view that they had at that time.

Blinded

Then we read, in verse 5, the answer of the apostle to these godless forgetters. He said, 'But they deliberately forget.' This can be translated, 'Willing this, they forget' – that refers back to the thought of the previous verse, that everything goes on in the same way as it has from the beginning of creation. And, 'willing this' to be the case, this is what they really want to believe, and because they really want to believe it, then they forget. This is in line with Romans 1 – their minds are blinded and they do not want to face or admit the truth, and so they are left to their own devices and live in the light of their false conclusions. False conclusions about the truth, about the way of the world and the way of the Universe can be fatal: 'they deliberately forget' or 'willing this', they 'forget that long ago by God's word the heavens existed and the earth was formed out of water and by water. By these waters also the world of that time was deluged and destroyed. By the same word the present heavens and earth are reserved for fire, being kept for the day of judgment and destruction of ungodly men' (vs. 5–7).

This godless mindset has blinded them to the evidence, preventing them from contemplating the possibility, let alone the certainty, of a coming day of judgement. And yet, two thousand years later, with all the advances of human science, no scientist on earth can explain or replicate the origin of matter or, despite recent hysterical claims to the contrary, the origin of life. And you can always hold on to these two things – whenever people talk about the way the world came about and all these amazing theories that scientists are coming up with – what about the origin of matter? What about the beginnings of life? Any serious scientist will have to admit they have no answers here; these things remain in the province of God alone. God alone can create. There are no human answers without God.

Sin and judgement

How were things brought into being? They were brought about 'by God's word', as indeed the opening chapters of the Bible inform us. Peter says, 'Do not say God did not intervene; he intervened at the creation in this dramatic way, and also the creation was followed by another great supernatural act: the judgement of sinful humanity by the Flood.' Verse 6 should really read, 'Through which the world of that time . . .' It refers to these two things: the word of God and the waters. God's word employed water to form the land masses of the earth in the creation and God's word again employed water to destroy the wicked at the time of Noah. Peter says, 'You have already got two great and obvious examples of what has happened in the past. Why then should anybody in his right mind deny God's promise of a final judgement to come?' The only difference between the final judgement and the judgement in Noah's day is that this final judgement will purge the *whole Universe*. In other words, in a sense, the judgement in Noah's day was a dress rehearsal for the great final judgement which will take place on a far greater scale. It is going to affect the whole cosmos.

Remember how the apostle Paul in Romans 8 tells us about the way in which sin has affected the whole creation, how it is in bondage to decay and how it needs to be released and how, when Christ returns, that release will come. There is going to be a universal cleansing and purging and the only other difference is that, this time, the chosen instrument of the word of God will not be water but *fire*. Fire purges and cleanses, just as water does. This is Peter's argument. He says: 'This Universe is not simply the product of chance forces, it is not progressing aimlessly.' Which is what the false teachers want to make you believe: 'Nothing is going to change, the world just rambles on. Presumably it will go on forever and you can

just live as you want because God really does not care.' That is why it
is so good to come to the Bible because it reveals the linear progres-
sion of history towards a very certain goal. It has a beginning and an
end.

It is why I love Ecclesiastes. Ecclesiastes chapter 1 talks about the
meaninglessness of life and the vanity of everything. Then it talks
about a life lived without God: 'What does man gain from all his
labour at which he toils under the sun? Generations come and generations go, but the earth remains for ever. The sun rises and the sun
sets, and hurries back to where it rises. The wind blows to the south
and turns to the north; round and round it goes' (vs. 3–6). It then talks
about the great water cycle: 'All streams flow into the sea, yet the sea
is never full. To the place the streams come from, there they return
again. All things are wearisome' (vs. 7,8a) and so on. The writer of
Ecclesiastes is talking about a cyclical view of life which has no beginning and no end and no meaning. God's nowhere to be found – so
different to the world and life that is described in the rest of the Bible.
People need to be woken up to the fact that there was a beginning
– it is why creation is important as a doctrine – and to understand that
there is a great end coming. This world will not go on in this way forever. There is a final judgement; that is the importance of biblical theology.

Forgetfulness of the godly

Verse 8: 'But do not forget this one thing, dear friends' – he is now
turned from the godless to 'dear friends', or rather, 'beloved'.

> Do not forget this one thing, beloved: With the Lord a day is like a
> thousand years, and a thousand years are like a day. The Lord is not slow
> in keeping his promise, as some understand slowness. He is patient with
> you, not wanting anyone to perish, but everyone to come to repent-
> ance. But the day of the Lord will come like a thief. The heavens will
> disappear with a roar; the elements will be destroyed by fire, and the
> earth and everything in it will be laid bare.

Even in Peter's generation, believers were inclined to listen to the false teachers because they thought Christ's return was long delayed. Jesus had spoken about these things; he had a series of parables in Matthew chapters 24 and 25 in which we learn that the protagonist, the master or the bridegroom, is going to stay away a long time. Peter could have employed the stories that Jesus told which have this repeated theme of the fact that the master is away a long time and people are doing all sorts of terrible things because he is away: the parable of the wicked servant who behaved so atrociously that the Lord branded him a hypocrite and sent him to hell (Matt. 24:45–51); the story of the foolish virgins who 'became drowsy and fell asleep' because 'The bridegroom was a long time in coming', and were shut out of the wedding banquet as a result (Matt. 25:1–13); and the people who had talents and needed to spend them wisely (Matt. 25:14–28).

Peter could have recalled these teachings, they would have suited his purpose, but he preferred, in this passage, to remind his beloved of a gospel reason for Jesus' apparent delay. If there were people, just a few years after the ascension, who were concerned at the apparent delay of the Lord Jesus Christ, it is little wonder there are vast numbers of Christians two thousand years later who are wondering whether the Lord is literally going to come back.

Here is the answer Peter gives them in verse 9. He says, 'The Lord is not slow in keeping his promise, as some understand slowness. He is patient with you, not wanting anyone to perish, but everyone to come to repentance.' The Lord's 'delay', he says, is not the consequence of unconcern, it is not that he is busy elsewhere and one day is going to wake up and say, 'For goodness' sake, I have forgotten about the earth! Time to go back.' It is not like that at all, although from Jesus' parables and stories, you might have got the impression the Lord might have been thinking like that! No, he has been concerned for us all the time, he has been dealing with us all the time, he has been active all the time in this gospel age, waiting for people to come to repentance so that he can bring all his elect into his kingdom. He wants heaven to be flooded out, super-crowded. He is longing for that.

Indeed, that is the character of God; he has always been patient in this way. Look at what Peter refers to, the Flood, that first judgement.

He describes Noah in chapter 2 as 'a preacher of righteousness' (v. 5). He was preaching the gospel; he was saying there is a judgement to come. For 120 years Noah was preaching the gospel and the Lord waited while the ark was being built. What about the whole story of Israel, with all their sin? How patient is God throughout the whole history of the Old Testament with Israel! How patient has God been with you and with me, after all our failings?

Like a thief

The Lord does not look at time as we do. Verse 8, 'With the Lord a day is like a thousand years, and a thousand years are like a day.' 'Don't forget,' says Peter, 'God stands outside of time. He is in eternity.' This is why he does not change, because change requires space and time; he stands outside of that. He has all the time in the world. So, Peter says, instead of being concerned about *whether* Jesus will return, accept that he must and start thinking about the fact that he is going to come back *unexpectedly*. We are told here in verse 10, 'like a thief', which is a strange image. We can understand Jesus being described as a good shepherd or as a bridegroom but to hear Jesus described as a thief is a bit much, isn't it? But we are able to take one aspect of that image – the image of the thief who comes unexpectedly and who catches us unawares. Jesus used this image of himself and it is so striking – it is an image that is used to wake us up.

Are we prepared for the Lord Jesus Christ to return? Are we prepared for that great day of the Lord? 'Oh yes, but these things have got to happen and so and so has got to take place and all these signs and so on.' Look, all of these signs that we are told about that must come before the return of the Lord; they are going to happen extremely quickly. Are you ready for the return of the Lord? If you have this doctrine of the return of Christ firmly in your mind, then you must strive after godliness and holiness, otherwise you are more guilty than those who dismiss it. If you sin against the light, then you are worse than the false teachers and the false prophets who had dismissed the light in the first place. If you accept the light but you say, 'Yes, Christ is coming back, but I am still going to live as I like' then that is the worst possible condition to be in.

'Listen', says Peter (vs. 11–13)

> Since everything will be destroyed in this way, what kind of people
> ought you to be? You ought to live holy and godly lives as you look
> forward to the day of God and speed its coming. That day will bring
> about the destruction of the heavens by fire, and the elements will melt
> in the heat. But in keeping with his promise we are looking forward
> to a new heaven and a new earth, the home of righteousness.

If we are true believers, we should be longing for his second 'appearing' (2 Tim. 4:8) – just as there were godly believers who longed for
his first. Remember we have nothing to fear. The Judge of the wicked
is the Saviour of the righteous. He is coming as the lover of our souls,
he is coming as the bridegroom of the bride. Let's look forward to the
wedding day of the church of Jesus Christ if we are part of that true
church.

The hope to come

The tragedy is that contemporary evangelicalism, in the West at least,
is so obsessed with the small deposit of God's blessings that we have
in this present world that we have deprived ourselves of this great
hope that is to come – when, by God's amazing grace, we shall rise up
with glorified bodies, see the king in all his beauty and share in his
glory and rule in a renewed and righteous Universe. It disturbs me
when we have meetings where we are encouraged to be satisfied with
so little and where superlatives are used about our present condition.
We are experiencing just the smallest deposit. We are not being
ungrateful when we say to God, 'I am so looking forward to the rich-
ness that lies ahead. It is going to be so much greater than now!' We
mustn't deprive ourselves of the joy and comfort of the Christian
hope.

Hope, along with love and faith, is one of the three great motiva-
tors of the Christian life. It is one of the three great engines that drive
the vessel through the water. When Paul writes to the Thessalonian
Christians, the first thing he thanks God for in them is their work,
which is the product of *faith*, and their labour, which is the product of

love – the labour of *love* – and their *endurance*, which is the product of their great *hope* in the return of the Lord Jesus Christ (see 1 Thess. 1:3). If even Christ needed the joy to be set before him in order to endure the cross (Heb. 12:2), how much more do we need this great incentive? Perhaps we live in a generation of people who do not endure in their Christian professions primarily because we have lost the great hope, and it is not preached as much as once it was.

Evangelism and prayer

Let's 'look forward to the day of God and speed its coming' (2 Pet. 3:12). How do we speed its coming? Jesus said, 'This gospel of the kingdom will be preached in the whole world as a testimony to all nations, and then the end will come' (Matt. 24:14). So let's preach the gospel to all nations. Evangelism is one of the answers to the question, 'How can we speed the coming of the Lord Jesus Christ?' Please let our evangelism be full of the returning Son of God and of the day of judgement. I have a problem with a lot of manuals on evangelism that appear today which tell you, 'You have got to be very careful what you say to unbelievers and there are certain doctrines that you soft pedal.' These New Testament believers did not have the advantage of some of these manuals and they just went for it. They told those who needed the gospel the things that had brought them to Christ.

One other thing that we do to speed the coming of Christ is prayer, and we will end on this note. Do we not pray, 'Your kingdom come' (Matt. 6:10)? Will that not speed the coming of the Lord Jesus Christ? I very much hope so. Do you remember some of the final words of the Bible where Jesus himself said, 'Yes, I am coming soon' to which we must respond in prayer: 'Amen. Come, Lord Jesus' (Rev. 22:20)? Do you remember the closing words, near enough, of Paul when he writes to the Corinthians and uses the Aramaic word – the very language of Jesus himself: '*Marana tha*' (2 Cor. 16:22), 'Come, Lord Jesus'? That term was probably a greeting that was used by early believers. We have lost this in our greeting of one another. Let it become a greeting once again. *Marana tha*!

I will build my church!

by Steve Brady

Steve Brady

Steve Brady was born in Liverpool where he was converted in his teens, is married with two children and three grandchildren and has been in full-time Christian ministry for over thirty years. He is Principal of Moorlands College and a Trustee of Keswick Ministries. He is the author of the Keswick Study Guides to Colossians and Galatians. A keen sportsman and author, he hates gardening and still has an irrational attachment to Everton Football Club!

Steve Brady preached at the evening meeting that was recorded for later broadcasting on BBC Radio 4, and this chapter is his sermon, shorter than usual for the radio.

I will build my church!: Matthew 16:18

Mission Statements! Don't you just love them? It seems like every organisation these days has to have one. Usually, they are concise statements of purpose that everyone on the team, at least theoretically, is supposed to understand. Some are highly memorable: 'To enable improvements in patient care,' may be a hospital's. 'To provide investors an attractive return through sustained growth,' may be a company's. Colleges like mine use them too: 'Moorlands College exists to equip people, passionate about Jesus Christ, to impact the church and the world.' The statement of a friend's church uses only ten words: 'To see lost people become committed followers of Jesus Christ.'

In Matthew 16, following immediately on from Peter's great confession – 'You are the Christ, the Son of the Living God,' Jesus responds: 'You are Peter, and on this rock I will build my church, and the gates of Hades will not overcome it'. Here is Jesus Christ's great mission statement. It is highly intentional: 'I will build my church!'

The Lord's commitment to the task

At the time when Jesus uttered those words, perhaps in the shadow of the shrine dedicated to the Greek god Pan in ancient Caesarea

Philippi, the idea of his establishing a 'church' – that is, a new community of his people, who would march to a different drumbeat, transformed by his grace and empowered to live in a different way – must have appeared ludicrous. Especially so, for a few verses later, Jesus speaks of his impending death. But herein lies the great secret of the church's future growth and development. For the one who in a short while will die on a cross, giving his 'life as a ransom for many' (Matt. 20:28), in the same breath speaks of his resurrection – 'he must be killed and on the third day be raised to life' (v. 21).

If he truly is the Son of God, as Peter and Christians confess, then his resurrection has an inevitability about it. 'It was impossible for death to keep its hold on him', as Peter will put it in his sermon on the day of Pentecost (Acts 2:23). Founders of companies, organisations, universities and nations rarely live long enough to see even a small amount of the fruit of their endeavours. But as Jesus commissions his people, in the final verses of this gospel, to take his good news everywhere, he promises to be with them always, because he is the Risen One, our great and available contemporary.

Conflict

So, in the light of that commitment by Jesus, all is going to be easy for the church, isn't it? Hardly! Jesus immediately mentions 'the gates of Hades'. In essence, that phrase represents death and anything and everything that gets in the way of his coming kingdom: his righteous rule that brings forgiveness to us, peace with God, and new life and hope to a world full of misery, pain, injustice and death. So, in a word, he is speaking of conflict: different kinds of opposition to his mission.

Sometimes, opposition comes from outside forces. I recall a beautiful young Welsh girl, Mary Fisher, a fellow student and friend, when I was training for the ministry. In the 1970s, she served as a teacher with the Elim Church's Overseas Mission in the Vumba Mountains in what is now Zimbabwe. And one terrible, evil day, 23rd June 1978, a dozen of her fellow missionaries and their children, along with Mary, were brutally massacred by self-styled paramilitary 'freedom fighters' for no other crime than following Jesus and seeking to serve their fellow human beings in his name. An army chaplain friend was part of the party who came upon this macabre and brutal massacre. He told me that the air hung heavy with evil and, as if in protest, all the animals and birds had fled from the area. When they checked Mary's cassette player, there she was teaching young children to sing some words of the apostle Paul, set to music: 'For me to live is Christ, to die is gain'.

When those terrorists were subsequently captured, my chaplain friend was there as they sneered and boasted about their crime. He told me how he wanted simply to get out a sub machine gun and exact revenge there and then. Instead, those men were shown something of the grace and love of Jesus Christ, leading at least one of them to repent, seeking Christ's mercy and forgiveness for himself.

At other times, the opposition comes from within the very church Jesus promised to build. Sadly, there are always churches of whatever denominational label that simply do not want to change or be changed by the power of Christ – they become stuck in some selfish time warp or ghetto. Likewise, individual Christians can peddle their own agendas, and personal stubbornness can get in the way of the will of God. Instead of 'seeking first God's kingdom,' it seems preferable to protect our own little fiefdoms. When I was a child, in my native Liverpool, I remember how many times my Mum would warn my sister or me, when we were pulling faces, 'Stop that, or you will stick like that one day!' The great news of the gospel is that no church or individual needs to 'stick like that' and stay as they are. Jesus comes to make 'everything new' (Rev. 21:5).

Confidence

What hope then for the church, when its battles are against the proverbial 'world, flesh and devil'? These words of Jesus – 'the gates of Hades *will not overcome it*' are the answer. The famous eighteenth century philosopher, Bishop Joseph Butler, when offered the Archbishopric of Canterbury, turned it down because he believed it was 'too late to try and support a falling church'. That was in 1747. By the end of that century, however, multitudes in Great Britain and America had joined the church of Jesus as waves of revival swept over those nations.

The following century, John Geddie left his pastorate in New London, Canada, and headed for a cannibals' island in the distant Pacific. His mission was so successful, and the love of the islanders for him so great, that years later a plaque was unveiled on the wall of his mission church on Aneityum Island. It said

> When he landed in 1848
> There were no Christians here.
> When he left in 1872
> There were no heathen.

In the mid-twentieth century, the Chinese Church was about one million strong when China underwent its Revolution. Today, that church is numbered in its tens of millions. All over the world, sometimes with just a handful of people, at other times in their thousands, Christians gather to worship and serve the Lord. How come? Because Jesus said, 'I will build my church.'

In spite of all the church's idiosyncrasies, hypocrisies and the sometimes shocking behaviour, and the failure of individual Christians and churches, in the face of all the challenges from different forces – economic, religious, scientific, political or whatever – Jesus promises to accomplish his purpose, calling people like ourselves – people in need of his love and forgiveness, transformation and empowering – to be part of his mission to his world, echoed in the prayer he taught his disciples 'Thy kingdom come, thy will be done on earth as it is in heaven.'

Remember that old 'Wayside Pulpit' challenge? 'Carpenter from Nazareth seeks joiners.' We are still invited to join. 'Come to me,' says Jesus, 'take my yoke upon you.' Be changed, be available, get involved in the action – 'and you will find rest for your souls' (Matt. 11:28f). The Mission Director awaits our response.

Living in the light of the future

by Hugh Palmer

Hugh Palmer

Hugh Palmer was a student when he became a Christian through the witness of a friend. His ministry has taken him from Norwich to London and Sheffield before becoming Rector of All Souls Langham Place since 2005. Hugh currently chairs New Word Alive. Previous responsibilities have included directing the Northern Cornhill Training Course. Hugh is married to Clare and they have three grown up children. He is a lifelong supporter of Brighton and Hove Albion Football Club.

Living in the light of the future

by Hugh Palmer

Hugh Palmer

Living in the light of the future: 2 Peter 3:14–18

He lay there, shot but not badly wounded, his gun on the floor beside him. He stared at the cop in the doorway, trying to work out whether it was worth reaching for the gun. In the doorway – Clint Eastwood, 'Dirty Harry', the brutal detective with his own strong sense of justice. His eyes narrowed, and he said, 'Go on, punk, make my day.'

We have got a day of justice in mind tonight but it is not Dirty Harry's. It is what Peter calls 'the day of the Lord, the day of God' in this chapter. It is even more lifeshattering than anything Clint Eastwood has concocted. Just look at 2 Peter 3:10: 'But the day of the Lord will come like a thief. The heavens will disappear with a roar; the elements will be destroyed by fire, and the earth and everything in it will be laid bare.' But, for all of that, there is a very different tone to Peter's voice than ever Clint Eastwood mustered. As Peter keeps saying to his readers, 'Go on, dear friends, make God's day.' That is where Jonathan left us on Wednesday night: our eyes on Christ's coming, looking ahead to that day which will change everything and bring in a breathtaking future; living as those with a stake in it. Peter is anxious we should not miss out. 'Beloved, dear friends' – he says it three times in this chapter – 'make God's day', 'be a part of God's future'.

Live looking forward

Look back to verse 12: that day will bring about the destruction of
the heavens by fire, and the elements will melt in the heat. He cannot
spell out more thoroughly that it will mark the end of this world as
we know it. 'But', verse 13 goes on, 'in keeping with his promise we
are looking forward to a new heaven and a new earth'. Not angels,
harps, clouds and white nighties. The other morning, Don Carson said
that if that was what heaven was going to be like, he did not want to
be there. It is the kind of rash, throwaway promise you can only afford
to toss out if you already know that God's word has guaranteed it will
not be like that.

There is a far more substantial, solid future ahead than that but we
have let people who have not read their Bibles shape our idea of the
Christian heaven. Cartoonists influence us more than Scripture; we
have a whole new creation ahead to enjoy. You see what he tells us
about it, right at the end of verse 13: it is the home of righteousness,
it is where all injustices have been righted, where wrongs and evils and
hurts are banished, where imbalances – social, economic, ecological –
have been removed, distortions ended. The home of righteousness,
where you will be godly and at home – where it will actually be cool
to be godly! It will not draw a sneer from the family, you will not get
a contemptuous smirk at work, you will not be left marginalised by
friends or society. And, if that thought draws no more than a passing
nod, barely a flicker of excitement, it is either because you are not
converted yet or because we have grown too comfortable in that
Western bubble of safe Christianity.

I think of a good friend of mine, a concert musician. She came over
to this country to train and she found Christ here. But she comes
from a country where the authorities do not look kindly on
Christians. I said, 'What's going to happen when you get back and
they discover you are Christian?' She said, 'Well, I do not know for
sure. It may be nothing but it might be – I mean it is happening to
others – it may be that, because I am a musician, they will break my
fingers.' Can you imagine living your Christian life with that in the
back of your mind all the time, and then discovering that ahead for

you is a home of righteousness? Peter's point, in writing, is that we should be part of that future. God's heart desire for you and for me is that we should enjoy that day. Go on dear friends, make God's day.

There is going to be some pragmatist who is going to ask the boringly obvious question; how? Peter puts it this way: 'Live looking forward.' Three times, in as many verses, Peter urges us to do just that. Did you spot back in verse 12: 'as you look forward to the day of God'; verse 13: 'we are looking forward to a new heaven and a new earth'; and then, in our section, right at the very beginning there in verse 14: 'So then, dear friends, since you are looking forward to this.' Live looking forward.

Changing values

Scoffers keep accusing us Christians of being out of touch and behind the times and sometimes we are, but the New Testament urges us to be living for the future. And what does that kind of living look like? Not waiting endlessly looking at your watch, not peering wistfully out of the window every few minutes wondering if the weather is breaking or Christ is coming. No, he goes on to explain: 'So then, dear friends, since you are looking forward to this, make every effort' – live with sleeves rolled up – 'make every effort to be found spotless, blameless and at peace with him.' Values will change on that day. Currency changes, so to speak. We know that currency changes when you cross a border; you can find yourself in a country where the pound sterling or even American dollars will buy you nothing.

I came across a great story about the Titanic. As the Titanic was going down and people were heading for the lifeboats, one lady rushed back to her state room, ignored jewellery worth thousands of pounds and just picked some fruit from a bowl on the dressing table. Where she was going, diamond necklaces were worth nothing but apples and oranges could be priceless in a lifeboat. What a change of values a day can make.

On that day, the day of the Lord, we would give millions for holy and godly lives that are at peace with Christ. It is the currency of heaven; 'make every effort to be found spotless and blameless' like Old Testament sacrifices. There, if someone, something, was going to be dedicated to the Lord, it needed to be absolutely perfect, not reasonably good.

Living at peace

I have been around enough years to see some trends. I do sometimes fear that the evangelical world hardly pays lip service to this idea any more. I know that we overdid it, we had our petty legalisms, and you can find bits of the evangelical world where these things are still alive and kicking. But there was also a zeal and a devotion that would never have allowed us to grow as careless as many of us have become about what we watch – the films, the TV, that Christians fill their minds with. What about how much we drink – I do not mean how many litres of water, but the alcohol? Are we careless about how scrupulous we are about our integrity at work or what we do? How careful and generous we are with the enormous amount of things we have, compared with generations before? To encourage moral carelessness – it is a bit like the scoffers of Peter's day.

I know I am sounding old and past it, and I remember hearing people say things like that to me when I was younger. Folk will come up and say, 'You need to fix your ideas, they are Victorian' to which, if I am feeling sparky, I will say, 'I hope not! I sincerely hope they are a lot earlier than that. I am aiming to be first-century radical.' But Peter actually says something slightly different. He says, 'Look, do not be behind the times, just make sure you are ahead of the times.' The glory days are not behind us. Please do not mishear me, do not think I am echoing back to some wonderful days like the fifties, which were nothing like as wonderful as we imagine they were. They are not the glory days, the glory days lie ahead. Live looking forward, let the day decide.

If Jesus came back and found you doing, saying, watching something and it would leave you embarrassed or ashamed, don't do, say or watch! A friend of mine has got a saying: 'If it will not do then, it will not do now.' It is a great rule of thumb. These false teachers are described by Peter as, 'blots and blemishes' in the previous chapter. I take it you and I do not want to be spiritual zit-heads on that day. 'Make every effort to be found spotless, blameless and' – notice how verse 14 finishes off – 'at peace with him.' Don't let us reduce this to moralism. Do not divorce it from our relational link to Christ, a relationship founded on, rooted in, the cross, maintained as we live looking forward, our hopes fixed on the coming Lord, who will have the last word on us all. 'At peace with him.' It does not save us from many painful hurts in this world, but it still changes everything.

I think of a youngish man who had been shabbily treated by the firm he had served loyally for a number of years. He said to me, 'Hugh, I cannot explain it and it would not do me or my blood pressure any good to fret over it, but he is coming and Jesus knows and, if it is of any account, on that day he will vindicate me.' It is a great thing to be able to say, isn't it? 'He is coming and I am at peace with him.' What a world of cancerous bitterness that can heal me from, what a hope to take into the darkest tunnel. He is coming!' What a must for that day, to be at peace with him. It might be despised and mocked and ignored now. It will be priceless currency then, to be at peace with him – and he is coming. So stay ahead of our time. Live looking forward.

Remembering the future

Here is the other way that Peter puts it. He says, 'Remember the future' which, if you think about it, is a very strange thing to say. 'Discover the future' perhaps, but how can you remember what is still to come? Only if you are a Christian really. Only if you already know the future and know how it is going to end, and why it is taking so long to get there. So you see verse 15 begins 'Bear in mind', not 'Get your mind round this' but 'Keep what is already there in mind.' 'Bear in mind that our Lord's patience means salvation.' He is referring here, I am sure, to the long delay before Christ's coming. He has mentioned it before, back in verses 8 and 9 and he comes back to it again as, no doubt, the scoffers are mocking the idea of his coming. We know their voices today: 'Pie in the sky when you die. The opiate of the people. Oh, I used to think that way myself, but now I have grown out of it. I have come to realise it is just a way of speaking, a style of writing to depict a spiritual thing.'

'Bear in mind,' says Peter, 'the delay means salvation.' We ought to actually remember it because we have experienced it. Let me put it this way: if the Lord had come five years ago, would it have been too early for you? Ten years, twenty years? Thank God he is patient, not wanting anyone to perish, but that everyone should come to repentance.

Peter's readers also know this point because Paul seems to have written to them as well. Look at verse 15: 'Bear in mind that our Lord's patience means salvation, just as our dear brother Paul also wrote to you with the wisdom that God gave him.' We do not seem to have that letter but it does not really matter because, verse 16: 'He writes the same way in all his letters, speaking in them of these matters.' So really you can take your pick of any one you have got. Remember the future. You know it. Keep it in mind.

Twisting the text

Peter almost stops here, as if he wants to show his readers the scenery in a little more detail. Only when you get out of the coach to look at the view can you discover that you have been taken to what I can only call an ugly spot rather than a beauty spot. You see how he goes on. Verse 16: 'His letters contain some things that are hard to understand.' We can smile at that, can't we? There are times when we know exactly what Peter means. Next time your home group gets a headache with some meaty chunk of Romans, which they've made heavy weather of all evening, just to cheer you up, think of Peter up in heaven with a little smirk on his face saying, 'Told you so!'

'His letters contain some things that are hard to understand, which ignorant and unstable people distort, as they do the other Scriptures, to their own destruction' (v. 16). Paul's writings are on a par with 'God-breathed Scripture' but notice this, these scoffers, these teachers, do not ignore the Scriptures – they know they cannot afford to. You'll come with your Bibles open, wanting to make sure you are being taught the word of God. No, they do not ignore Scripture, they distort it, they twist it like a rope. 'It is all right. The preacher used plenty of Bible texts.' Yes, but so I suspect did these preachers. They used them and then twisted them like torturing someone on the rack until they can be made to mean what they couldn't possibly have meant to the writer.

It goes on happening today, doesn't it? It is not just the authority of Scripture that comes under attack, or its sufficiency, but its clarity. You come to an ethical issue and people always seem to be muddying the waters, straightaway: 'Are we sure the Bible means that? Couldn't it mean this as well? In their times, didn't they understand that?' Or those in more academic circles keep asking, 'Can we possibly expect to understand the writer's meaning in a text? We have just got a reader's interpretation. and isn't one reader as good as another? There is no objective meaning to a text we can hope to find.' Peter says, 'There are clearly some wrong ones.' When you come down to street level and you come into the home group Bible study circles, it comes out in the way people speak very often: 'Ooh, what this bit means to me is . . .'; 'I like to think of this verse as . . .' They never seem to ask the question: 'What did Peter mean by . . .? What did Paul mean by . . .?'

We may have to sweat because he can be hard to understand, but genuine disciples will get there. They certainly will not distort the meaning. We cannot make the Bible say anything other than Christ is coming and we are to live for then, now. 'Well,' says someone, 'that is all too complicated for me.' 'Your future is at stake,' says Peter, 'so wise up.' Do not let the scoffers talk you out of your future. Bear in mind – because it will not naturally stay there – the urgency of the here and now. The scoffing of the cynics will make us forget, will put it on the backburner. Remember the future.

This is Keswick, you know about false teachers. But if you read on here, you discover Peter is writing to the converted. Isn't that what verse 17 says? 'Therefore, dear friends, since you already know this' – he is writing to Keswick – since you already know this, do not put your feet up: 'be on your guard so that you may not be carried away by the error of lawless men and fall from your secure position.' And it happens so easily. For some it is battle fatigue. They are weary of always being the odd one out, but he is coming. For others, it is doctrinal doubt. All the unpopular implications of his coming get pushed down the priority list, but he is coming. For others, it is lifestyle choices. I was told earlier this week of a senior Christian leader I know a little bit who has just left his wife of many, many years, and taken up with his PA. He has forgotten his future. It is possible, if you sit him down and ask him the doctrinal question, 'Is Christ coming again?', he will say, 'Yes, of course' but he is not living looking forward, is he? Remember your future. He is coming.

Growing in the grace of God

Just before we end, there is one little note Peter wants us to know: you guard all of this by growing, not by putting locks on it, not by retreating into a Christian ghetto. Notice verse 17, 'be on your guard'. Verse 18, 'grow in the grace and knowledge of our Lord and Saviour Jesus Christ.' I do not grow by standing still: 'I am on good firm ground here, I will just stay exactly where I am.' I do not grow by building up a library of Keswick ministry books on my shelves. No, I guard it by growing. Not by resting on what I have learnt, but by growing in grace and knowledge. It is how we begin our Christian lives, and some of you have got a pretty long lifetime ahead of you to discover the riches of God's grace, to get to know him through and through and through. Don't fall into the trap of looking back to see how far you have come. That is the way to plateau. We live looking ahead to that day.

Others of you, you are on the other end of the age scale. Some of you I am grateful for. I feel young! Even though there are years and years of Christian experience, there are still new experiences ahead. I remember a very godly man, not too far back, talking with him. He is almost ninety now. He is frail and life has closed in on him. He has gone from being housebound to almost room-bound, experiencing a dependency on others that is foreign to him. And, as we were talking about how he is and how he copes and so on, he said to me, very movingly, 'Hugh, I hope, by the grace of God, to end well.' But he is travelling in unchartered waters and growing in the grace of God.

There was a veteran French climber. He had led many an expedition, and he died after a fall in the French Alps. They buried him close to where he fell. He has just got a simple cross on the grave and on it is written this: 'He died climbing.' It is a great epitaph for any Christian, isn't it? 'He died climbing.' 'She died growing.' How God would love to say that about each one of us. That would make his day.

Conclusion

Let us think over what we've heard tonight. There are priorities that may need reorientating; remember your future. There is a lifestyle that may need changing; live looking forward. You may have attitudes that will need altering; make God's day. Let us pray for the Spirit's finger to come on the hurt, the wrongdoing, the carelessness. Make every effort to be found spotless and blameless and at peace with him.

Valuable trials

by Jonathan Lamb

Jonathan Lamb

Jonathan Lamb is presently Director of Langham Preaching for Langham Partnership International, a global programme seeking to encourage a new generation of preachers and teachers, networking with national leaders in many parts of the world. Jonathan serves as Chairman of Keswick Ministries. He is a member of St Andrew's Church in Oxford. He is married to Margaret and they have three daughters.

Valuable trials: 2 Corinthians 1:1–11

I wonder if you know the story of the missionary Evelyn Harris Brand, the mother of well-known surgeon Paul Brand. She was brought up in very well-to-do English family, but she gave it all up and went to India as a missionary. After ten years of service her husband died, and she came home a broken woman. But a year later, she went back and poured her life and soul into the hill people with whom she had worked. Philip Yancey recounts how she was involved in 'nursing the sick, teaching farmers, lecturing about guinea worms, rearing orphans, clearing jungle land, pulling teeth, establishing schools, preaching the gospel'.

She lived in a portable hut eight feet square. At 67 she fell and broke her hip, and her surgeon son came and urged her to retire. She'd already broken her arm, cracked several vertebra and had recurrent malaria. But she said to him: 'Why preserve this old body if it is not going to be used where God needs me?' And she died 28 years later at the age of 95, buried in a simple cotton sheet by the villagers. This is what a co-worker said: 'Granny Brand was more alive than any person I have ever met. By giving away her life, she found it.'

Granny Brand is an example of a Christian life which comes right out of the letter of 2 Corinthians. It is very different from what we might call the 'what-is-in-it-for me' spiritualities. Many modern spiritualities are very human-centred, concerned with self-fulfilment and self-realisation, and this can sometimes influence Christian attitudes too. We expect the Christian life to fulfil us, to meet our needs. In fact, some have been known to teach that a Christian who is facing hardships or trials must be outside of God's blessing; surely true faith overcomes the hurdles and the difficulties, and means we should be riding high on a success-orientated spirituality?

Of course, that misses the emphasis of vast sections of the New Testament, not least the letter of 2 Corinthians. For Paul, at the heart of the Christian message and at the heart of all Christian service lay a painful paradox. It is summed up in the Lord's words to him in 2 Corinthians 12:9. 'My grace is sufficient for you; for my power is made perfect in weakness.'

This word from the Lord represented an important breakthrough for Paul. He came to understand his weakness in relation to the gospel message which he preached. What was the gospel after all? It was God at work through the weakness of the crucified Jesus, God's power displayed in the apparent weakness and foolishness of the cross. So it was no surprise that the gospel should reach the Gentiles through the weakness of the messenger.

What Paul came to understand was that, in carrying out God's work, human resources have their limits. And many here this evening have come to realise that too. We can look at the size of the task, and compare that with the resources at our disposal; we can look at the opposition that we encounter; we can become weighed down not only by the burden of human need all around us, but with our own feelings of inadequacy, doubt, or frailty.

Paul had been pushed to the limits of his endurance, as he explains in the catalogue of sufferings in 2 Corinthians 11. His missionary work was quite literally killing him. But he had come to understand that it was precisely at this point that God's power was displayed. He had understood his weakness in relation to the theology of the cross. His struggles were a mark of true discipleship, the result of fellowship with Christ. That is why he could boast, 'when I am weak, then I am strong' (12:10).

As a young Christian I contracted polio and, as part of his encouragement to me to see this in perspective, my father gave me a simple illustration: Christians are like tea – their real strength is drawn only when they get into hot water. That sums up the theology of 2 Corinthians. So the theme of chapter 1 is the key to understanding the whole of Paul's letter. The opening thanksgiving represents a trailer for the main feature film which is to follow.

Paul was under attack by some in Corinth who doubted that he was a genuine apostle, and already in verse 1 he has stressed that his calling is from God: 'an apostle of Christ Jesus by the will of God'. He defends the integrity of his ministry as an apostle by showing that suffering is part of authentic Christian service.

In these verses there are four reasons why trials are valuable, and they apply to all true disciples today.

1. We share Christ's life verse 5

You'll notice the frequency of the words 'trouble' (three times), and 'suffering' (four times), and they are found throughout the letter. Trouble describes pressure of various kinds. One form of ancient torture was to place a large boulder on a person's chest, a crushing pressure that squeezed the life out of him.

But notice that Paul deliberately and graphically connects those sufferings with Christ: 'For just as the sufferings of Christ flow over into our lives, so also through Christ our comfort overflows' (v. 5). Suffering is an inevitable result of being united to Christ. It is a natural and normal part of life for Christians. Paul develops the idea in chapter 4, where he says that his experience is a reflection of the dying life of Jesus. 'We carry around in our body the death of Jesus' (v. 10); 'we are given over to death for Jesus' sake' (v. 11).

Paul is saying that he is sharing his master's earthly experience. Four times in those two verses (4:10,11) he refers to 'Jesus' the man. And the word he uses in verse 10 could better be translated 'we carry around in our body the dying of Jesus'. When you read some of his catalogues of suffering you can understand this – at times he probably looked just like someone in the process of dying, someone in the process of being crucified. So if you are a Christian, united to Jesus

Christ, there is no avoiding this weakness. We should suspect all models of the Christian life which try to avoid this identification with Jesus' suffering.

And here in chapter 1, he is making the point: far from being evidence of Paul's lack of spirituality, or casting doubt on his leadership, suffering was a badge of his discipleship. It was a clear indication that he was fulfilling his God-given ministry in serving Christ. 'The sufferings of Christ flow over into our lives.' Of course, this verse certainly does not imply that Christ's sufferings in securing our redemption need extending or completing through the experience of Christians. Christ's suffering was unique, complete, and once and for all, as Paul explains in his letter to the Romans. No, Paul is describing the intimate relationship between Christ and those who bear his name. Our life is his life.

Many years ago I was thankful to have met Dr Helen Roseveare, who served as a medical missionary in what was then Zaire and spoke here at Keswick in the 1970s. During the revolutions of the 1960s she faced beatings and torture and rape. She tells in her writing of an occasion when, as she was close to being executed, the Holy Spirit reminded her of her calling. She writes: 'Twenty years ago you asked me for the privilege of being a missionary, the privilege of being identified with me. This is it. This is what it means. These are not your sufferings; they are my sufferings. All I ask of you is the loan of your body.'

She was spared execution and later wrote: 'He didn't stop the sufferings. He didn't stop the wickedness, the cruelties, the humiliation or anything. It was all there. The pain was just as bad. The fear was just as bad. But it was altogether different. It was in Jesus, for Him, with Him.'

It is no wonder that Paul 'boasted' about his weaknesses. The more he suffered, the more it was evidence of the privilege of being identified with Jesus Christ. The same argument of solidarity with Christ appears in the second part of verse 5. If we are united with Christ in his sufferings, then through Christ we will also experience something else in our lives. And it is the second reason why trials are valuable:

2. We experience God's comfort verses 3,4

In fact, notice that he begins the section with a great note of thanks-giving in verse 3: 'Praise be to the God and Father of our Lord Jesus Christ, the Father of compassion and the God of all comfort, who comforts us in all of our troubles.'

This is not the power of positive thinking. Paul needed more than this. The ability to praise God in the midst of pressure can come only from an experience of God's strengthening comfort. The key word 'comfort' is found ten times in five verses. The same word describes the Holy Spirit's ministry in John's Gospel. The Spirit's ministry is to draw alongside, to strengthen us and equip us when we are tested. No matter what pressure or affliction we might suffer as Christians, this is more than matched by God's strengthening presence.

This happened time and again for Paul, and it is true for you and me. I can imagine many here being able to testify to this reality: that however dark the night or however ferocious the storm, God does not abandon us. Do you remember when Paul finally arrived in Rome, at the end of his life, sitting in a Roman dungeon, cold, lonely, deserted, close to martyrdom, he wrote to Timothy: 'But the Lord stood at my side and gave me strength.'

Sheila Cassidy tells the story of a Bible found in a detention cen-tre in Chile. An unknown Christian, the victim of the secret police, had written inside: 'I could only close my eyes and hold his hand and grit my teeth and know with cold, dark, naked knowing that God was there.' The Dutch Christian Betsie Ten Boom in the Ravensbruck concentration camp said: 'We must tell people that there is no pit so deep that he is not deeper still.'

We need this word of encouragement, because many of us face demanding pressures and carry some very heavy burdens. The costs of discipleship are very real indeed. Something hits us, and it is not easy to sustain our trust in the Lord. So we shouldn't miss this comforting cer-tainty which runs right through the Bible. 'Even though I walk through the valley of the shadow of death, I will fear no evil, for you are with me.'

Paul refers to the source of that comfort in three phrases in verses 2 and 3. Just as grace and peace come 'from God our Father and the

Lord Jesus Christ', so our comfort comes from 'the Father of our Lord Jesus Christ, the Father of compassion and the God of all comfort'. They are great descriptions of the God who cares. They're not simply technical or religious phrases, but they describe a profound intimacy with God. It is true for all Christians: we often come to know our Father best through suffering.

So, first, we share Christ's life, second, we experience God's comfort; and the third reason why trials are valuable is this:

3. We help God's people verses 4,6,7

If we are united to Christ, we are therefore united to one another. Christians are bound to Christ and bound to every other believer. So there is a community dimension to Christian experience, including our experience of suffering and comfort.

'We can comfort those in any trouble with the comfort we ourselves have received from God' (v. 4). As we experience the Lord standing alongside us in times of pressure, so we become qualified to bring encouragement and help to others. We might not experience the same pressures and troubles as others, but that does not limit our ministry. The experience of comfort itself is the basis for helping others. We are able to help one another 'in any trouble' (v. 4).

Notice in Paul's case it is more than comfort and encouragement. Verse 6 says 'If we are distressed, it is for your comfort and salvation.' He says the same in chapter 4: 'So then, death is at work in us, but life is at work in you' (4:12); 'All this is for your benefit' (4:15). His experience of dying actually serves to bring life and salvation of the Corinthians. They are the beneficiaries of all that Paul went through. 'All this', he says, 'all I am going through – is for your benefit'. Weakness in our service can be for the eternal benefit of those whom we serve. So verse 7 demonstrates that both suffering and comfort are part of Christian fellowship. 'You share in our sufferings, so also you share in our comfort.'

Paul is absolutely certain that they will experience God's care which will sustain them in their difficulties. In verse 7 he describes his hope for them as 'firm', it is secure and reliable. The God of all comfort will never fail them.

When we are under pressure it is never easy to have the presence of mind to assess objectively how God has helped us. But it is good to remember that, when the pressure is on, God can redeem those experiences, and can use them for his good purpose of strengthening others in the Christian family. The theme is also picked up later in this section. Paul not only acknowledged his dependence on God in verse 9. He also affirms his dependence on God's people: 'as you help us by your prayers' (v. 11). Once again Paul is underlining the importance of Christian community. God had delivered him, but that was a direct result of their prayers for him.

Our prayers for each other achieve something in God's hands. Paul was not too proud to acknowledge that as an apostle he was in desperate need both of God's help and of their prayers. To pray, he implies in verse 11, is to work with God in achieving his purpose – 'as you help us by your prayers'. And he links prayer with thanksgiving. The more prayer there is, the more God's people everywhere will join in praise at what God is achieving.

So we share Christ's life, we experience God's comfort, we help God's people: and the fourth and final reason why trials are valuable is this:

4. We trust God's purpose verses 8–11

One of the reasons we have difficulty in understanding the idea of 'valuable trials' is because we have what might be called a Santa Claus theology, where we imagine God is a warm, loving, celestial Father Christmas, characterised by indulgent benevolence. David Pawson once wrote

> I once knew a family in which the children were never punished. No matter what they did, from smashing windows to painting the cat green, it was excused as childish exuberance or legitimate self-expression. I must admit at times I envied them. But what those parents were

offering their children was not love so much as sentimental indulgence. Yet that is what many people think God offers us.

But that is how we react isn't it? 'If God loved me he wouldn't let this happen.'

In verse 8 Paul describes the hardships he had suffered in the province of Asia, and although the detail of that suffering isn't clear, its severity certainly is. For two years he struggled to proclaim Christ in a context of active opposition from others, whether from occult forces, from those with a vested interest in other local deities, or from mob violence.

So he tells us openly both of the unbearable pressures and of the ways in which God met him. He is remarkably honest in describing his experience. Verses 8 and 9 are very striking: 'We were under great pressure, far beyond our ability to endure, so that we despaired even of life. Indeed, in our hearts we felt the sentence of death'. As JB Phillips paraphrases it: 'We were completely overwhelmed, the burden was more than we could bear; in fact we told ourselves that this was the end.' Paul felt as if the waves were crashing against the bows and he was close to sinking.

These raw wounds are here for a purpose. Why was this happening to a supposed man of God? Why was God allowing him to go through such experiences of despair and deep depression? Paul explains it in verse 9: 'But this happened that we might not rely on ourselves but on God, who raises the dead.' That is God's purpose. Throughout the letter we find that God takes us through these afflictions in order to bring us to a recognition of our own helplessness, to bring our self-confidence to an end, and to teach us an exclusive trust in God. In desperate times we learn to hold him fast.

If we didn't face these challenges we would so easily revert back to living independently of God. Apparently William Wilberforce used to have a small stone in his shoe to remind him to pray. Almost every step reminded him to depend on God. God's purpose in our lives is not to bypass difficulties but to transform them. He does not beam us up, magically removing us from the pressures, but instead uses those very events to expose our complete inadequacy and to demonstrate his complete reliability.

In verse 9 Paul not only describes the life-threatening experience, but he underlines that God can be trusted as the one who 'raises the dead'. Although he had written to the Corinthians about the doctrine of the resurrection in his first letter, here he is describing not a future hope but a daily reality. And this is why we have chosen 2 Corinthians, as this week we consider the theme of Christ-centred renewal. We are united to Jesus Christ in his death but also in his resurrection life. It is there again in chapter 4: 'we are given over to death, so that his life may be revealed in our mortal body' (4:11).

The resurrection is not confined to a future life beyond the grave; it is already a part of our experience. Our life is bound up with his. God can raise up Christians who, like Paul, are despairing of life itself. Because God had delivered him from 'such a deadly peril', Paul knew God could be trusted for further deliverance, now and in the future: 'On him we have set our hope, that he will continue to deliver us, as you help by your prayers' (v. 10).

Of course, it is only a partial deliverance. We will one day face death itself (though with the same hope of resurrection to which Paul refers). But we can look to God to keep us safe from death while he still has work for us to do. We do not know if our lives will be short or long, sorrowful or joyful. But our lives will not end until God chooses that they should. I often take comfort from a poster I was given when I was younger. 'God placed me on earth to complete a certain number of things. Right now I am so far behind I will never die.'

So in the despairing moments in our lives we should learn to trust God's purpose, to trust the God of compassion and resurrection. He will not let go of his hold on us. He is the one who can be trusted to deliver us now, in the days ahead, and on the final day of resurrection.

These then are the ways in which we are to understand our suffering. For all true Christian disciples, trials are extremely valuable. We share Christ's life, experiencing his suffering but also his resurrection life. We experience God's comfort as he draws alongside us by the Spirit. We help God's people as we share our suffering, our comfort and our prayers in the Christian family. And we trust God's purpose, which moves us away from self-reliance, independence, or even despair, so that we trust the God of the resurrection.

Priorities in Christian service

by Derek Tidball

Derek Tidball

Derek Tidball was Principal of the London School of Theology from 1995–2007. He has served as pastor of two Baptist churches, worked for the Baptist Union and was President 1990–1991, and became a Vice-President of the Evangelical Alliance in 1995. Derek has written over twenty books including *The Message of Holiness* in IVP's Bible Speaks Today series. Derek is married to Dianne, lives in Leicester and divides his time between theological education, writing and preaching.

Priorities in Christian Service:
2 Corinthians 4:1–6

Introduction

It never ceases to amaze me that in these days of the digital camera, when there are so many mega-pixels available and so many lenses and such brilliant colours, the old-fashioned black and white photograph still has its attractions and is a favourite. It reminds me of the old Kodak box camera I used to have as a child, that I lost on Weymouth seafront. There is some attractiveness about the simplicity of the black and white photograph, in contrast to the complexity of modern technology. That is the issue here: simplicity versus complexity. Black and white show in very sharp contrast the picture that you are looking at.

When we come to 2 Corinthians 4, the apostle Paul is showing in black and white terms a study of ministry, of Christian service, in contrast. He contrasts very clearly the normal worldly way of persuading people to follow a belief, and the alternative Christian way of serving Christ. There is an authentic ministry that belongs to those who have adopted an apostolic mindset and practice, and there are inauthentic ministries, who just cover secular leadership practices with a very thin veneer of Christian love.

It takes something to reconstruct our mindsets and to learn to serve God in such a radically different way. I am constantly encouraged by how slow the disciples were to pick up on the teachings of Jesus, and to reconstruct their thinking. James and John were still saying, well into the ministry of Jesus, 'Jesus, when you come into your kingdom, may we have the seats next to you on your throne?' – in spite of all that Jesus had taught about the greatness of being a servant. Peter in Gethsemane was still drawing and using the sword, as if Christ's kingdom had to do with military power and might. There the disciples were, as Jesus was about to depart, still saying in nationalistic terms, 'Is this the moment when you are going to restore your kingdom?'

Even after the day of Pentecost, Peter's mind in particular still ran along those old lines, that to be a true follower of God, you had to buy into all the customs of the Jews as well as have faith in Jesus Christ. When he has that vision on the rooftop in Joppa, he puts two impossible words together, as he says 'No' and 'Lord' in the same breath. He is either Lord and you say 'Yes' or he is not Lord, and you can say 'No.' It takes quite something to think, by way of contrast, about the style of service that God would call us to. Paul was constantly battling with the congregation that he founded at Corinth, as people infiltrated it and advocated old forms of ministry. In these enormously rich verses, we have a series of contrasts between old and new forms in ministry; inauthentic patterns and authentic God-given patterns of service.

Merit and mercy in ministry

The first contrast comes in the very first verse. I constantly go back to these words because I need to: 'Therefore since through God's mercy we have this ministry . . .' We live in a meritocracy. You have to have a certificate to prove you are capable of doing anything these days. Years ago I found my neighbour dead. She was an elderly lady who had pined for her husband, who had gone on before her. A workman came to her house and could not rouse her one morning, so came to me to ask whether I had seen her around that day. I hadn't, but I had a key, so we went in together and explored. I found that my neighbour had passed away overnight, in bed. The police came to take a statement from me, and I was speaking in ordinary language, so I said, 'I found that Mrs Dickens had died.' 'Oh', they said, 'you cannot say that. You are not qualified. Only a medical doctor can pronounce death.'

'I am not a medical doctor' I said, 'but I am a minister of religion, and I have met a number of corpses in my time. And I can assure you that that was one of them.' But I did not have the right piece of paper, the right certificate, so I was not qualified. There were peddlers of God's word in Corinth, as Paul refers to them in chapter 2:17, alternative preachers who wanted to say to the congregation, 'Paul does not measure up. He has not got the right qualifications. He cannot authenticate his ministry in the way that our contemporary culture requires.'

Paul begins by saying, 'It is not a matter of merit; it is a matter of mercy.' He could have trotted out his qualifications, as he does in Philippians 3. He had an impressive CV. His background, education, training and gifts were impressive. God had prepared them in his life, and was going to use them. But Paul knew that what qualified him for ministry was not his merit but God's mercy. He had already spelled it out (2 Cor. 3:5): 'Not that we are competent in ourselves to claim anything for ourselves, but our competence comes from God.'

It is staggering that he used the word 'mercy' as the basis for his ministry and service. Think of the word 'mercy' for a moment. Who receives mercy? The people who receive mercy are the guilty; the condemned; the failures; the hopeless. Others do not need mercy; they can get by on their own. Paul was desperately aware of another side of his background. Not only was he educated in Tarsus and a Pharisee: he had been a persecutor of the church: a murderer; a bigot; a torturer of the Christians. He was aware how he was arrested on the Damascus road, the experience that colours all this passage and that there, he had received mercy not only for sins forgiven but a call to Christian discipleship and mission.

Those of us in ministry may sometimes feel that the ministry we have received is a severe mercy, when we are battling up against things. But we need to stand back regularly and to reflect that it really is just mercy that qualifies us to serve God. The moment we begin to think God is fortunate to have us on his side, the moment we think that we are important, we have lost it. The only basis for serving God is mercy.

I know your churches do not think that, very often. They want you to merit your ministry. They want you to be as seeker friendly as Bill Hybels, as purpose-driven as Rick Warren, as doctrinally sensitive as John Piper, as able a communicator as Rob Bell, as respected by youth as Mike Pilavachi, as evangelistically effective as Nicky Gumbel. They want you to be all that, in yourself. Why cannot you do this? Why cannot you measure up to that? Why do you not read this? Why do you not go to that conference? Why do not you introduce that? Why isn't this programme in the church? It is all so often about merit, and we can sometimes buckle under that pressure.

Some of you are weary because you are labouring under other people's expectations. You need to remind yourself that you are not in Christian service because of your merits or to measure up to what others want. You are there by the mercy of God and that is sufficient. That makes serving God a gift, a response of gratitude, an act of worship. It means that serving God is never our possession or our right, it is not something we have to live up to. We are all failures, dreadful failures some of us, but we are there because of God's mercy. Paul never loses the wonder of that mercy.

Truth and spin

The second contrast deals with the style or method of our ministry. The way we exercise ministry grows very naturally out of the basis of our ministry, whether it is based on our own qualifications or simply wonder at the mercy that God has shown in our lives. Paul goes on to say that he had renounced secret and shameful ways and his style was to set forth the truth of the gospel, plainly.

We live not only in a world which is governed by meritocracy but we live in a world of spin. We encounter spin constantly in our politicians; the last government was commonly accredited with designing spin as an art form. Alistair Campbell justified much of it in his writings. 'You can put a positive gloss on things if it is for the general good,' he said. Peter Oborne wrote a book called *The Rise of Political Lying* in which he analysed the way Tony Blair, if he believed something, believed passionately it was the truth, whether it had any basis in fact. We know about the twenty-four hour news management that went on, the desire to bury bad news on certain days. It is sad because it breeds a mistrustful society.

Actually spin is not a recent invention. The ancient philosophers of Paul's day, the great entertainers, were masters of the art of spin. There are plenty of books written about the techniques of persuading audiences in the ancient world. Some favoured sensationalism, some favoured gentleness to woo your congregation along until they would agree to anything. Some talked about battering your congregation, whipping them into the position that you wanted. They talked about the different levels of arguments and the different kinds of speech that could be used to persuade people. Powerful oratory and exaggerated claims and persuasive gimmicks were all part of the world in which Paul lived. Now they are saying, 'Paul, one of the problems we see with your ministry is that you are not adopting those techniques. You are not manipulative enough, you have not compromised the gospel enough. Just tell us a bit so that you will win more converts, you can give them the small print later on.'

As James Denny said, summarising this passage, when these arts are looked at closely, they all come to this: the minister has contrived to put something of his own between his hearers and the gospel. Paul says, 'I am not going to do that, I am just going to tell it as it is without apology, without consumerism. I am going to set forth the truth plainly.' Brothers and sisters, you have to have confidence in the gospel to believe that it will work and, judging by the way much of the church in Britain behaves, we do not have that confidence. We very often want to keep the gospel back and hook people by other methods or messages first. But the plain, simple, steady teaching and exposition of the gospel, the unpacking of the unsearchable riches of Christ, are surely still the most persuasive way of bringing people genuinely to a point of conversion and discipleship.

Paul is fully aware of the reality of the situation. He says it may not be popular to do it this way but we do not distort the word of God. He will not shape it in such a way that it traps people, and then tell them the truth later on. He recognises it may not be successful. There are many people who will not obviously respond to the gospel this way because their minds have been blinded, they cannot see the truth of it though it is staring them in the face. It seems so obvious but there is some consumer resistance to it.

I have been, over the years, to many conferences on evangelism that have reduced evangelism to marketing. They suggest that, if only we get the right language, the right strap line, the right sound-bite, the right technique, if only we can tap enough into the culture, then of course it will be obvious, everyone will see the truth of the gospel and come to believe. But it does not work like that. We are not selling cars or soap powder. We are engaged in a spiritual battle and the god of this world has blinded the eyes of many and will prevent them from seeing what seems so transparently sensible and obvious to us. Telling the truth is not to be judged by its effectiveness or not.

Some years ago, Bishop John Taylor, the former bishop of Winchester, who had worked on the mission field for some time, wrote that we latter-day Christians are nervously anxious about the effectiveness of our proclamation of the gospel. The prophets and apostles were obsessed by divine revelation or the lack of it. 'We are obsessed,' he said 'by human response or the lack of it.' But when you have discovered the truth and experienced the mercy of God, as Paul had on that Damascus road, then that is what obsesses you and that is what you speak.

A ministry which speaks of Christ versus a ministry full of self

Don't we live in a self-absorbed society? I benefit enormously from Facebook and keeping in touch with many of my friends. I am glad to read many of the blogs that my friends are writing, but we are very self-confident as a culture at the moment, in downloading all our blessed thoughts and many of them not so blessed, onto the internet, thinking that everybody will want to read them. We love to impart ourselves all the time to all sorts of people. Sometimes preaching is like that, full of information about what the pastor has been up to that week, who they have visited and how busy and pressurised their ministry has been. We talk so often about ourselves that we hide the real truth that we are supposed to be talking about.

I am going to fall into my own trap here. Last week, my wife and I were on holiday in Spain and we did one of those things that I only ever do on holiday. We went on one of those trips to see a top rate horse riding stable, to see them training the horses for a top rate show. We went to this marvellous place but they seemed curiously reluctant to show us the horses. First of all, we were introduced to the gardens, which were magnificent, and we saw the lawn mower in action. Then we went into the marvellous old house and were taken through the rooms. We were taken to the horse riding museum to see the artefacts from the past, and we were, of course, taken to the shop. And this time, having looked at my watch many times to wonder when horses were actually going to appear, eventually we got to see the horses.

So many churches are like that. They hide Christ away; he is the after-thought. When we have hooked people with other things, maybe we will produce him and will talk a bit about him. No, Paul says, authentic ministry, the true priority in service, is not to talk about yourselves, who are merely servants, but about Christ as Lord. In fact, in these couple of verses, Paul uses some very very rich language about Jesus, who had walked on this earth not many decades before. Jesus, that man of Nazareth, what does he say about him?

The sovereign Lord

Paul is echoing language that Peter used on the day of Pentecost in Acts 2:36. 'God has made this Jesus, whom you crucified, both Lord and Christ.' He is plugging in to the constant Christian witness, the early apostolic testimony, that Jesus Christ, the man of Nazareth, was none other than Lord over all: pre-eminent, as Paul puts it, in the Universe. He was Lord over creation, Lord over Caesar, Lord over all hostile powers, Lord over the future, Lord over sin. 'Lord' because that is the language the Jews would have used for God. 'Lord' because he was none other than God himself and, in a world that so often seems to be out of control, when there are so many oppressing powers, we need to proclaim Jesus Christ as the sovereign Lord.

The crucified Lord

The language Paul uses echoes not just that message on the day of Pentecost in Acts 2, it picks up language that he had used in his first letter to the Corinthians, chapter 1:23: 'we preach' – what? – 'Christ crucified'. Not only the sovereign Lord but we preach a crucified Saviour. Death and resurrection are never far below the surface of 2 Corinthians.

The creative word

Paul's mind next goes to Genesis 1, to God saying, 'Let light shine out of darkness'. The New Testament picks up on that creative power of God speaking and things happening, and applies it to Jesus. John 1 says, 'Through him all things were made; without him nothing was made that has been made.' Colossians 1:16 says, 'All things were created by him and for him.' This great creative person, Jesus, who brought our Universe into existence and holds it still, not only created it in the first place but recreates society and individuals. And one day he will recreate the heavens and the earth. Light brings life and Jesus brings life.

The glorious image

We see the glory of Christ, who is, says Paul in verse 4, the image of God. In verse 6 he returns to it: God's glory displayed in the face of Christ; the invisible God is made visible in Christ, the glory which was marred at the fall in the Garden of Eden is seen in all its pristine beauty and unspoiled condition, in the person of Christ. 'We preach' said Martin Luther, 'always him, the true God man. This may seem a limited and monstrous subject, likely to be soon exhausted but we are never at an end of it.' Our message is Christ and our priority should be to speak of him.

Light and darkness

There is a fourth contrast in these verses. It is the contrast that Paul has been heading towards, which speaks of the result of our ministry.

Paul contrasts light and darkness in a way that we are very familiar with the apostle John doing, but he picks it up in his own way because his experience of light and darkness is shaped by encountering that blinding light on the road to Damascus. He reflects on that, as it governs all his priority and ministry. He talks about the way in which, in the world, there are blinded minds and darkened lives. The darkened world in which we live arises from minds that cannot see the beauty of Christ, who cannot see the glory that is shining out from him; minds that you could never persuade by rational argument, that need illuminating. Elsewhere Paul will tell us, and John will echo, these minds are darkened because of the sin in which people live and delight, that they do not want to give up. They are futile in their thinking because of their immoral and godless way of living.

We often say to people in argument, 'Surely you can see?' But their minds are made dull, as Paul said in the previous chapter, and remain blinded now to the truth of God. By contrast, there are not only blinded minds and darkened lives: there are illuminated hearts and transformed lives. At God's merciful and gracious initiative, he makes light shine, in our hearts, to give us the light of the knowledge of the glory of God. 'Knowledge' they used to say 'is power.' It is not so much power as there to be transformative. We have this encounter with God, we see the glory of God, not so that we may be superior but so that we might become changed and Christlike: so that that broken image, which is in our lives, corrupted by the fall, can be restored. We can become more and more like the image of God, that we see in Christ.

So we are back to where we began. It is all about grace and mercy. What are our priorities in Christian ministry? To live a life of mercy and to serve, not because of merit but because God, remarkably, has taken the risk of trusting us with the gospel. It is all about truth, not about spin and devising ways to persuade people. It is up to God whether they are converted or not, and we cannot do it. But it is about telling them the good news that we have found in Jesus, bringing light into a darkened world. It is all about Christ, he is central. We are called to integrity, to fidelity, to humility, as we serve Christ, and to let his mercy, which we have experienced, overflow into the lives of others.

I sometimes think the church is not particularly known for its mercy. It is known for its judgementalism, its respectability, its tut-tutting, its objecting to this, that and the other. The God in whom we believe is one who is merciful to the unkind and the wicked, as Jesus said in Luke's gospel. And that mercy is the only basis on which we can live, the only basis on which we can serve and the only message that we have, because of Christ, to convey to a watching world. May God grant us mercy, in our experience, in the face of the criticisms and the meritocracy that is required of us. May God grant us to speak truth and to forego spin. May God grant us to speak of Christ and not of self so that to him may be all the glory, Amen.

A matter of life and death

by Liam Goligher

Liam Goligher

Liam Goligher has been Senior Pastor of Duke Street Church in Richmond since April 2000. He has also pastored churches in Ireland, Canada, and in his native Scotland. His teaching is heard weekly on Premier Radio, Sky Digital and Freeview. His Duke Street ministry is available online. Liam is a Trustee of Keswick Ministries and is the author of several books including *The Jesus Gospel* and has contributed to a number of others. Liam is married to Christine, they have five children, three granddaughters and a Bedlington Terrier!

A matter of life and death:
2 Corinthians 4:7–15

Many of you will know that I live in Richmond, in the west of London. Richmond is a trendy London suburb where the rich and famous live, with one or two obvious exceptions. But my first impression of Richmond was not of that trendy London borough at all. I first went to Richmond on a Sunday morning to preach at the church there, and parked my car on Richmond Green, just a few yards from the church building, which is normally a very attractive place. On that Sunday morning, it was not very attractive at all. It was a Sunday after a Saturday when there had been a rugby game at Twickenham stadium. Whenever there is a game at Twickenham, Richmond is invaded. So that first morning, all you could see was rubbish everywhere, wherever you looked.

We live in a throwaway culture. There is packaging around takeaway food, the wrappers around chocolate bars, the bags we put our groceries in. Some things haven't changed in two thousand years. Two thousand years ago, you didn't have plastic bags but you did have the simple clay jar. That was about the nearest thing to a throwaway item that you could get at that time. It had no stand alone value, no significance of its own. Its significance came from what it contained; flour, olive oil or some seed. Sometimes its contents could be more exotic: the family jewellery was to be found in some of these clay jars. Archaeologists have discovered dumps of these clay jars at the edges of towns and villages, right around the ancient world, the kind of clay jars that the apostle Paul is referring to here. So it is no surprise that when Paul wants to have an image to describe the banality, fragility and brevity of human life, he should use the image of the clay jar. Whenever we read this section, that is the dominant image.

First century prosperity gospel?

Paul is answering his critics. They have complained that, when they look at him, there is nothing they could see in him that gave any indication of the importance of the message that he purported to proclaim. Their test of spirituality was that, if it was authentic, then it had to be marked by victory and prosperity: by a self-assertiveness and self-confidence that seemed to be lacking in the apostle. The people who were annoying Paul in Corinth were the ancient equivalent of the prosperity gospel people that we have today. That gospel appealed to the culture of Corinth. Corinthians had a cultural propensity to self-reliance and self-promotion. They had nothing to say to the weak, the insignificant, the people who were sick or dying, the powerless. All they had to speak were words to the rich and famous, the successful and the overcoming. Their picture of the victorious Christian life was of a trouble-free ticket, to a cross-free trip, to a this-world glory.

Paul says, in his letter, that the true gospel has something to say to those struggling with their own weakness and mortality, with sickness and death, with the skeletons in their cupboard. The true gospel has something to say to the people I know, people like me who know very well their own insignificance and ineffectiveness, their own record of weakness. The true gospel has something to say to people like you.

A paradox of Christian ministry

In the opening verse, verse 7, Paul begins with the word 'But'. In that opening conjunction, he is drawing a contrast between the *content* and the *container*. 'But we have this treasure in jars of clay, to show that the surpassing power belongs to God and not to us.' The paradox is simply this: the contrast between the message and the messenger, between a glorious Lord and an often inglorious church, between an Almighty God and a weak servant of the Lord.

Paul is following on from what he is just said in this chapter. He has been describing the *content* – the gospel of God. The gospel, he has been saying, is a gospel about God's mercy, God's grace. It is a gospel that comforts the comfortless; it is a gospel that saves the sinner; it is a gospel that brings change into our lives. He describes the gospel as a treasure. The Greek word gives us our English word *thesaurus*: something of precious and priceless worth, something to be prized and protected. The treasure is both the gospel and that which is contained in the gospel. The gospel is the announcement of what God has done in Christ for the salvation of his people. So the gospel is Christ in you, the hope of glory. The content is the gospel and the gospel is about Jesus. He is saying, 'We have this treasure of the gospel, that is Christ, in jars of clay.'

The content is the gospel of God, the container is the servant of God. See the contrast between the greatness of the divine glory of the knowledge of God and of the glory of Christ who is the image of God on the one hand, and the frailty and the unworthiness of the container in which it lives and through which it is manifested to the world.

We were in the States on holiday just a couple of weeks back and our oldest son and his wife and their daughter were with us. David's wife bought these glossy magazines and I looked at them. In these magazines were photographs of the stars, the rich and the famous, and descriptions of what they were wearing and how they kept fit. There is so much focus in our media, on the externals, the containers. The world is always interested in the classy container in which a human being is borne around.

Paul is making a contrast here between what is in the individual Christian – Christ in you, the hope of glory – and the rather worthless and weak container in which that is found. His enemies had contemptuously described his bodily appearance as weak and his ability in public speaking as being of no account. They hoped to discredit his authority by emphasising that the container in which the message was found was worthless and unworthy. But notice what Paul says here. The paradox is that, though the container is relatively worthless, the contents are priceless. The gospel treasure is indescribably valuable, and gospel people and gospel ministers are of little value in comparison. How does the paradox work? Notice how he puts it: 'that the surpassing power belongs to God and not to us'.

This idea of a clay vessel comes from the Old Testament where it is used in several places, and Paul picks it up in Romans, describing God as the Potter. God has made you, as you are. You, as a clay vessel, are not entirely worthless, you are valuable to God. And, although in the eyes of the world you may be worthless because of your appearance or afflictions, your inadequacies and past failures, to God you are valuable because he made you. Whenever that phrase is used in the Old Testament, it emphasises the absolute sovereignty of God and the fragile dependence of humanity upon him. We are nothing but we are utterly dependent on God.

So Paul pits together these two things: the fragility of the clay jar on the one hand and the surpassing power of God on the other. He says, 'Here you have these two things: one deficient, one efficient. And our deficiency is a challenge to the power of God, yet the power of God is such that not only does it match our weakness, it overcomes and overwhelms it. It exceeds our weakness and goes beyond it – to demonstrate that the power belongs to God alone.'

Ambrose, one of our church fathers wrote: 'By speaking of earthen vessels, he [Paul] signifies the infirmity of human nature, which can do nothing unless it has received strength from God; and God proclaims himself to his own praise through those who are weak, in order that the glory may be given to him, not to man who is formed from clay.'

This is how Paul sees the glory of God in Christ at work among the church. For many people in our day, the gradual moral transformation he mentioned earlier, the endurance in adversity modelled by these early Christians, seems too mundane to be miraculous. Yet the apostle asserts that it is precisely in this mundane process that God's almighty power is demonstrated today. Paul is speaking of himself as an apostle here but, by extension, what he says applies to every genuine servant of the Lord Jesus Christ. We are fragile in ourselves; relatively insignificant and unattractive in the eyes of the world. Yet God chooses to use weak vessels in order to keep us in our place, so that the excellency of the power may be of God and not of us.

Had God deposited his gospel in a strong and permanent body, it would have proved to be a fatal mixture for our proud and sinful nature. Satan, as God made him in the beginning, had enormous gifts. He was the first, the most beautiful and most powerful of all the angelic creations that God made. But he was lifted up with pride and he fell because of it. Often we wish we were better than we are, stronger than we are, but we do not understand our weakness. I remember, as a young man, hearing one of our great Scottish preachers quoting from an evangelist called Jock Troup: 'There are few men God can trust with power.' I imagine that goes for women too. If you know your own heart, you know that is true because within our hearts are the seeds of every form of rebellion, every form of pride. That reminder to us of our own frailty is constantly there to tell us, over and over again, that the power belongs to God and not to us. That is the paradox.

A principle at work

This is how Paul puts it

> We are afflicted in every way, but not crushed; perplexed, but not driven to despair; persecuted, but not forsaken; struck down, but not destroyed; always carrying in the body the dying (sic) of Jesus, so that the life of Jesus may also be manifested in our bodies. For we who live are always being given over to death for Jesus' sake, so that the life of Jesus also may be manifested in our mortal flesh.

His argument here is that if you are called to follow Jesus, you are called to follow a crucified Messiah. And, in following a crucified Christ, you are called to live a cruciform life. It is *endurance not deliverance* that is the mark of the supernatural in this world. That is the last thing you would think. You would imagine that, if the supernatural is going to be seen, then surely the supernatural has to be seen in miraculous deliverances, but Paul's argument here is that it is seen in endurance.

I remember reading a course that was widely used among Christians and discovering that, in explaining the Christian life, it had a chapter on *healing* but no chapter on *suffering*. However much you believe in healing – and I have seen God answer prayers for healing – all of us will suffer and few of us will be healed. If we are going to be honest with people who are considering Christianity, we had better own up about the cost of following Jesus, and the reality of living in a fallen world where Christians, like everyone else, take sick and eventually die.

Look how Paul explains the real miracle, the real work of God, in verse 11: 'For we who live are always being given over to death for Jesus' sake, so that the life of Jesus also may be manifested in our mortal flesh.' The doctrine he refers to is our union with Christ. Our close connection to him is a faith connection, a Spirit connection: we are placed into Christ Jesus by faith. That means that when Jesus died, we died with him. When Jesus, rose, we rose with him. There is this bond of life that unites the believer to the Lord Jesus.

Four times here in this passage, Paul uses, unusually, the name 'Jesus' – standing alone. Normally, Paul prefers to refer to 'the Lord' or to 'the Lord Jesus' but here he refers to Jesus, emphasising our Lord's humanity. He is saying that our lives are so bound up with him, there is no escaping this principle of dying and life: as verse 10 says, we are 'always carrying in the body the dying of Jesus'. I have done a bit of translation of my own here. I have not used the words 'the death of Jesus' (v. 10) because I think, in the original Greek, the inference is 'dying'. The apostle is referring to the whole way in which God works in dealing with the work of saving humanity.

How did the Lord Jesus come into the world? He emptied himself by taking on something he had not before, the form of a servant, in order that he might reach us. He did not even take on the image of a powerful, attractive, influential human being. Read Isaiah 53:2: 'he was despised and rejected by men' – 'he had no form or majesty that we should look at him, and no beauty that we should desire him.' There was nothing that would have made you think, when you saw Jesus walking down the street, 'There is a hunk.' He was not born into a palace, he did not come as a millionaire or go around the Sea of Galilee in a speedboat. The humanity that Jesus took was nothing special in its outward appearance and, throughout his life, there is this dying. He laid aside everything that human beings consider powerful in order to do the most powerful thing imaginable; to reconcile rebel sinners to a holy God.

See how Paul describes the experience of the Christian. 'We are afflicted' he says, talking about himself and us. To be afflicted means 'to be hard pressed' or 'weighed down'; to feel the pressure crushing us. This verb refers to any physical, psychological or spiritual pressure that we may feel. It is a catch-all word. There may be something in your life that is pressing down upon you. It may be a physical ailment; the anxiety of a diagnosis; a child who is giving your heart pain; those skeletons in the closet that you wish you could forget; or depression and anxiety. You may ask, 'In what sense is that the dying of Jesus?' It is in this sense: while someone who does not believe in the Lord Jesus may suffer similar things and may ask the question 'Why?', they do not expect an answer. There is no one *to* answer. The affliction is worse for you because you are a Christian. You know God has the power to stop it. It is exacerbated by the very fact that you believe in the Lord Jesus.

Look at the next word: 'perplexed'. You could translate it 'bewildered but not desperate'. It means 'to be at a loss'. Have you ever faced some crisis in your life or some issue in your heart, and you do not know what to think or how to respond? Then Paul moves on to 'persecuted'. The word was used of chasing an animal, or of an enemy who was hunting you down. It is often used in the psalms, as King David described himself being hunted like a wild animal by his enemies. Paul knew what this was like. We know what persecution is, though it is more subtle here in the Western world. It is the snigger you get when you are asked what you have done over the weekend, or the sarcastic tone in which people talk about religious things when they know you are overhearing. You can feel like stranger in your own land, a foreigner among your fellow countrymen because of your allegiance to King Jesus. Persecution is a day to day experience and, in other parts of the world, some of our brothers and sisters are experiencing it full on.

Then Paul uses the words 'struck down'. The word means to be thrown down, like being tossed down in wrestling or knocked out in boxing. It describes the very extremity of suffering, where it seems as if that is it, finished. Paul is saying here that these things were gradually killing him. Every difficult experience left him weaker, more vulnerable than the one before. Every recovery was like a resurrection from the dead. He was experiencing 'the dying of Jesus' in the shape of affliction, bewilderment, persecution and humiliation (vs. 8–9), but each time he goes on to speak of the life of Jesus, in those four 'but not's. Notice that the deliverance there is not *from* suffering but *in* suffering. There is a discovery that, in each extremity, there is the help of God. God perseveres with his people – 'afflicted but not utterly crushed'.

People have said to me, 'I feel as if the pressures are just crushing the life out of me, that there is no place left for faith or confidence.' I have said to them, 'But you are breathing and you are speaking and you are talking about the things of God. You think you have lost it all together but you are concerned about it. Isn't that the evidence there is still life there? It may be nearly gone but it is not finally gone. You are persecuted but not forsaken.' That is the same word that Jesus uses on the cross, when he cries out in dereliction: 'Why have you forsaken me?' Paul uses it about a friend called Demas: 'Demas has forsaken me, having loved this present world.' Friends might forsake you, your spouse might forsake you, but you will never be utterly forsaken. God will never forsake his people. He will never desert his chosen ones.

Paul speaks of being struck down, but not destroyed. These verses are teaching us that God perseveres with his people, and he keeps with us. He does not beam us up out of the problem. Remember *Star Trek*? 'Beam me up, Scotty?' – and you are out of trouble immediately? There is no beaming out of trouble in the Christian life but, in it, God perseveres with his people. The principle is that we are always being given over to death for Jesus' sake. These things are part of the divine plan, not coincidence or accidents. They have not taken God by surprise. God has written the script for your life. You may not be totally happy with everything that is in the script but you do not know the conclusion yet to the story.

> When through fiery trials my pathway shall lie
> Your grace all sufficient shall be my supply
> You'll strengthen me, help me, and cause me to stand
> Upheld by your mighty omnipotent hand.

The purpose at work (vs. 13–15)

Paul states two reasons for these trials that we face in our lives: something that happens in us and something, ultimately, that goes to God. God is working a spirit of faith in us, and he is doing it for his own glory, the glory of God. 'Since we have the same spirit of faith according to what has been written, "I believed, and so I spoke," we also believe, and so we also speak' (v. 13). Paul is reflecting on what he has just being saying. When he talks about a Spirit of faith, he is not thinking about mental assent to the truth of the historical facts of the gospel, nor is he talking about faith as if faith in itself has some kind of energy that stands alone. Faith is not a magical formula designed to get things from God. Faith is resting totally upon God, receiving from God the mercy that is in the Lord Jesus. Faith always rests upon God, always receives from God, all that God has promised to give.

Paul is saying where we are most likely to see the Spirit of faith in the world. Do you see faith at work when things are going smoothly and well in your life? When do you really find yourself giving yourself to prayer? Isn't it when something disturbs the even tenor of your life? Isn't it then that the faith, that is still in there, emerges to the surface, as you call on the name of the Lord and cast yourself on his mercy? It is in the place of pain that we discover that we are resting on Jesus.

What is Paul saying here, in verse 14? 'Knowing that he who raised the Lord Jesus will raise us also with Jesus and bring us with you into his presence'. What is he trusting in? He looks to the gospel events, the resurrection of the Lord Jesus, and he reasons from that event to his experience, and to the experience of Jesus' people, and says; 'If God raised Jesus and God has promised that I am in him and share something of his suffering (not his redemptive suffering but his serving suffering), then I can also, one day, share in his resurrection. God will do for me what he has done for Jesus.' God raised Jesus, he will raise me. That is what Paul believed, that is how faith argues.

He is saying, 'The God who raised Jesus will raise us up also with Jesus.' And what will he do when he raises us? He will present us, with you, in his presence. Why? Because he has undertaken to do so.

All of this, Paul goes on to say in verse 15, has an impact on other people. When they see you struggling yet still believing, they are encouraged. I remember a lady once saying to me: 'I have been coming to the church and I have been watching you. You really are quite an inadequate man, aren't you? But it has actually helped me to see that if God can use people like you, he might be able to use people like me as well.' The principle that Paul is teaching here is 'For it is all for your sake, so that as grace extends to more and more people, it may increase thanksgiving, to the glory of God.' For Paul, the glory of God was everything. The glory of God was the goal, that God should be praised because we prize him above all things, because his praise and glory is the chief end of our lives. It is the great purpose of our existence. And how does glory come to God? Glory comes to God when, in the weak, insignificant, broken lives of people like you and me, people see reality.

Do you remember the story in the Old Testament about Gideon and his men? They were faced by a greater overwhelming power. Yet he whittled down his army, just to the few, and gave them each a clay water jar and told them to conceal in it a flaming torch. They crept up on the enemy at night then, at a given signal, smashed the jars and waved the torches. The enemy was scared, turned on themselves – great strategy – and the Israelites won.

Do you feel that you are too common, too weak, too shy, too inarticulate, too damaged, too disabled, too afflicted to be of any use to God? Do you know what you have? Thelma Howard died in 1981. For twenty years of her life, she had been a maid for a couple called

Walter and Lillian. Every Christmas, Walter called Thelma into his study and gave her a Christmas card, and in this card there was an official-looking bit of paper. Year by year, she took it home and put it in a box under her bed and, when she died, she died in poverty. When they came to sort out her possessions, they found that box under her bed and in the box they found company stock worth about £8 million ($12 million). Thelma Howard was a millionairess and she never knew it. For twenty years she had been a maid to Walt Disney and his family.

Do you know what you have? Do you know what God has put in you; the one in whom are hid all the treasures of wisdom and knowledge; the Father's beloved Son? He is going to take that clay jar, that body of yours, that is one day going to dissolve to dust and bring back together the pieces of that body and so transform it that, one day, that clay jar will be shown off to the Universe as a magnificent object in which the glory of God shines. The dying of Jesus will be followed by the life of Jesus and glory will be yours, for Jesus lives and reigns supreme, and his kingdom is still remaining.

Commendable living for a commendable ministry

by Joe Stowell

Joe Stowell

Joe Stowell is the President of Cornerstone University in Grand Rapids, Michigan. An internationally recognised conference speaker, he has also written numerous books and works with RBC Ministries in Grand Rapids, as well as having his own web ministry. Joe serves on the Board of the Billy Graham Evangelistic Association and Wheaton College, and has a distinguished career in higher education and church leadership. Joe and his wife, Martie, are the parents of three adult children and ten grandchildren.

Commendable living for a commendable ministry:
2 Corinthians 6:3–10

Introduction

There are certain circumstances in my life that are dangerous to me spiritually. One of them is counters at airplane terminals, when they cancel my plane or when they say it is delayed and I am going to miss where I am going, or when my seat assignment is changed. You wouldn't want to be around me when those kinds of things are going on.

I think my all-time horror story was when I was pastoring in a small town in Indiana. I was asked to speak at a conference on expositional preaching, about two hundred miles away to the north. I was so excited about the opportunity. The town was called Kokomo, Indiana and we affectionately called the little airport Kokomo International Airport. I called the travel guy and said, 'Does anything fly from Kokomo up to Michigan?' He said, 'Yes, there is a commuter plane. It starts in Indianapolis, goes to Kokomo, then to South Bend, then to Grand Rapids.' I said, 'I need to be in Grand Rapids by ten o'clock.' He said, 'You can catch the seven o'clock plane.' I said, 'Great, sign me up.' As he was signing me up, he said, 'By the way, you need to know these are tiny little commuter planes and, if the weather's bad, they might just skip Kokomo.' I am the eternal optimist. I said, 'No problem.'

I remember driving out to get to the plane on the morning appointed and I did notice that the cloud cover was a little low, but I didn't think about it. At Kokomo International Airport the ticket-taker, the air traffic controller and the baggage person are all the same guy. I remember walking in and handing him my bag and my ticket. He said, 'By the way, this weather's kind of low today, I am not sure this plane's going to get in.' Right away, I could feel something tightening up, deep down inside. I said, 'Hey, I am speaking to a thousand people at ten o'clock this morning. You have got to get that plane down.' He said, 'We will try, but I cannot guarantee it.'

While he was talking to me, he morphed into the air traffic controller right before my eyes, and he started talking to the pilot. The pilot was approaching and the pilot said, 'We are going to give it a try but I do not know if I can get it down.' I was all over this air-traffic-baggage-ticket-taker guy: 'You tell him, he has got to get it down, I have got to get to Grand Rapids!' He said, 'Hey, people on that plane have to live.' I said, 'I don't care. Get that plane down!' I heard the engines get louder and louder and then they got softer and softer and I heard the pilot say, 'We are on our way to South Bend.' I said, 'What am I going to do?' He looked at me and said, 'You are a minister, aren't you? God will take care of you.'

I have thought about that situation often and I doubt if, right then, I would have been able to say, 'Hey, can I talk to you about the transforming power of Jesus Christ?' What a scary thing, that God has trusted the ministry of his word and the transforming power of his gospel to frail, fallen, failing people like me.

I remember a seminarian asking me, 'What is the most important thing in ministry?' I told him, 'The way you live your life.' If we live our lives wrongly, it gets in the way every time. And that is why in our text tonight, Paul is commending his life as a life that has been lived with the dynamics that have facilitated the ministry of God, and not obstructed and damaged it. God has trusted that to all of us, in our little jars of clay. What Paul is going to tell us is this: that there are three dynamics to a life that commands itself to keep the ministry commendable. Firstly, that we live no-fault lives, secondly that we live no-fault lives as servants, and thirdly that we live no-fault lives as servants who endure regardless. Let's use the measurement and feel the Holy Spirit call us to these dynamics in our own lives.

Living the no-fault life

In 2 Corinthians chapter 6 we see the first dynamic when Paul says, 'We put no obstacle in anyone's way, so that no fault may be found with our ministry' (v. 3, ESV). Paul is very much aware that the most important thing is the facilitation of the ministry of God through his life, and that everything else is dispensable, to keep the ministry fluid. This may be a reference to when he came to serve in Corinth. He did not ask for them to support him, but made tents and worked so that they would not think that he was just in it for the money.

I thought about obstacles that easily get in the way of our capacity to facilitate God's work through us. I came up with a short list. I thought about material things, like what we wear. I have a passion for really cool cars. I work for a Christian University that thrives on the donations of God's people, so I decided not to drive those kinds of cars. Or if we go to a restaurant, we always over-tip. We want them to know that Christians may be the most generous people they've had in their restaurant.

It is usually in the small, silly things where we get our practice to do what is right, or in the words that we speak. Are you involved in gossip and slander with your neighbours, when you are the representative of Jesus Christ? Did you ever think that you are barricading your capacity to ever reach them for Christ? Maybe it is work, your job, when you are part of the grumpy group which does not like the company and which complains about the boss. Or you are the person who does not work hard. Did it ever cross your mind that perhaps you are barricading the ministry of God through your life?

For those of us who are in the ministry, it is probably one of the laziest places you can be. As a pastor, you spend all your times at Starbucks or on the golf course or whatever and people say, 'Doesn't this guy have a job?' I decided one day I was going to buy a boat and name it *Visitation*, so when they called the office, my PA could say, 'Oh, he is out on *Visitation*.'

Sometimes it is our freedoms in Christ. I realise there are always discussions about should Christians drink wine or shouldn't they drink wine. I have a hard time defending not having a glass from Scripture, although there may be other reasons. There may be times when I think I might have that freedom, but taking that freedom might be a great obstacle in another person's life – someone who maybe does not believe they have that freedom. What is more important to you: the facilitation of the gospel, or exercising your freedoms?

On a daily basis, we make choices about facilitating the gospel through a life that is lived without fault. Part of the problem is that you and I may be thinking, 'Hey, I am not perfect; doing this no-fault kind of life . . . I cannot be perfect, I am going to blow it.' I would hate to tell you the catalogue of the ways I have blown things, but there is a biblical mechanism to keep you in that no-fault zone.

Early on as a pastor in my first church, we had a Sunday school superintendent, but we did not have a big staff, so I was still doing all the jobs. I remember one Sunday morning, I walked past him and he said, 'Hey, pastor, don't forget to order the new Sunday school material for the next quarter.' I said, 'Fine, I'd be happy to.' He said, 'We need it in a week and a half.' I totally forgot it. The next week, it was the same scenario, same Sunday school superintendent. I walked by him and he said, 'Pastor, did you order the Sunday school material?'

It was not even premeditated. I said, 'Yes!' and as soon as the word was out of my mouth, I knew it was a problem. I walked into my office and I thought, 'Forget it.' Then the Holy Spirit showed up and he said, 'So you are the truth teller this morning in the pulpit, are you? You just lied to them.' 'Ah, no, actually it was not premeditated. It was just kind of a slip.' 'No, I think it is a problem and you need to do something about it.' At which point, flesh appeared on my desk, saying, 'If you admit that, you will lose your job. You'll never recover. Not only that, you can call FedEx tomorrow morning. It will be here by Wednesday and nobody will know.' Then the Spirit said, 'Well, actually, I will know, God will know, and you will know.' So I said, '1 John

1:9: "If we confess our sins, he is faithful and just to forgive us our sins and to cleanse us from all unrighteousness." Dear Lord, that was such a mistake. I did lie. I have sinned. Please forgive me.' He did and then he said, 'Go talk to them.' Flesh said, 'You do not need to do that. You just got cleansed.' God said, 'You have got to make it right with those people.'

I went out and called them in. I said to them, 'God has called me to be your pastor, and that means I shepherd you and support you and live an exemplary life. I have just failed you miserably. I want you to know I didn't order the material and, when I told you I did, I lied to you. I was wrong and I want you to forgive me and pray for me, that my life will grow and become more solid and more what God wants it to be.' Then there was this pause, but eventually the man said, 'Pastor, of course we forgive you. Nobody's perfect.'

Humbling yourself and making it right is so powerful in a relationship. It is possible to be living in the no-fault zone.

The no-fault life as a servant

Paul calls us to live in the no-fault zone as a servant. He says, 'so that no fault may be found with our ministry, but as servants of God we commend ourselves' (v. 3). I find it fascinating that Paul, holding the highest position in all the apostleship, the highest position in the church, consistently refers to himself as a servant, and sometimes as a slave. We do not like being called to be a servant; we do not like 'downstairs'. We want to be 'upstairs' people. Yet God calls us to that and Paul, in calling us to live like Christ, calls us to live like servants as well.

Philippians 2: 'Let this mind be in you which was also in Christ Jesus who, being in the form of God, [having all the prerogatives of God at his fingertips] decided to pour himself out and chose to be a servant.' Can we imagine that? Can we get our heads around the fact that the Almighty God could have chosen anything for his life? It would have been right for him to go to Jerusalem and set up a throne, bedeck himself in beautiful robes, with a brilliant crown, with valuable jewels, with trumpeters hailing his arrival, demanding that everybody come and pay homage to him with expensive gifts. He is God. Will we ever get used to the fact that when Jesus landed on this planet, voluntarily, he chose to be a servant? He calls us to be servants, and it is a struggle. I think the struggle is best seen in the lives of the disciples, as Jesus is constantly trying to teach them the ways of the kingdom.

In Matthew 20, James and John come to ask Jesus a favour. They are asking Jesus if, when the kingdom comes in, they can be the two big shots. But what really is fascinating is that they bring their mother to ask the question. So get the picture: James and John standing on each side of their mum, who approaches Jesus and says, 'Sir, grant that these, my two sons, might sit the one on your right, the other on your left, when you come into the kingdom.' She was asking for the big shot spots in the kingdom. Those were the ones that had the ear of the king, had the limelight, the leverage, the power. I do not think James was there saying, 'Mum, I have been with him for two years, he does not like questions like that. Do not ask that question.' I think James was probably saying, 'Mum, I don't think he quite heard that, ask it again.' The reason I think that is because the story goes on to tell us that when the other ten disciples heard this request, they were moved with indignation (v. 24).

Why do you think they were so ticked off? They wanted it too and these guys had beaten them to it. Here you have twelve, minus one, of the most dedicated people this world has ever known and, after these years with Christ, still down deep inside is this demon of 'I want to be on top. I want to be noticed. I want the applause. I do not want to be a downstairs person any more. I want to go up. I want to have power.' If those demons could be present in their lives, how much more in our own lives is this nagging sense of always wanting to be seen and applauded, and having a power position? Luke 22 tells us that when Christ was with them in the upper room, they were arguing about who would be greatest in the kingdom.

A life lived in the no-fault zone is really about a life no longer about you; a life about a willingness to serve others, a willingness to sacrifice for others. You say, 'I didn't get a thing out of the sermon.' Did it ever cross your fallen brain that maybe the sermon was not for you, maybe it was for Bob at the end of the pew? Did you ever think, 'Good, that sermon was for somebody'? Did it ever cross your mind that maybe you ought to pray for and encourage your pastor? Maybe we ought to serve those around us instead of grumping and complaining that somehow, life is no longer about me. It just makes so much sense that serving in the no-fault zone opens doors, facilitates ministry.

Servants who endure

No-fault servants endure regardless. Look at what Paul says: We live no-fault lives 'so that no fault may be found with our ministry, but as servants of God, we commend ourselves in every way: by great endurance . . .' What he is saying is that he has lived with comprehensive endurance. He has endured in the midst of trials, afflictions, calamities, beatings, imprisonments, riots, labours, sleepless nights, hunger. He has endured, so he says, 'by purity, knowledge, patience, kindness, the Holy Spirit, genuine love; by truthful speech, and the power of God; with the weapons of righteousness for the right hand and for the left.' So his virtue has remained steady and strong in the vacillating realities of life.

He says, verse 8, 'through honour and dishonour, through slander and praise. We are treated as impostors, and yet are true; as unknown, and yet well known; as dying, and behold, we live; as punished, and yet not killed; as sorrowful, yet always rejoicing; as poor, yet making many rich; as having nothing, yet possessing everything' (vs. 8–10, ESV). How many of you know that life runs like that? Back and forth and there is gravity in those polar things that tend to pull you off course. The praise tends to make you proud, and the slander tends to make you despairing and disappointed. He is saying, through all of that, 'I have not shifted, I have endured.' He has stayed the course.

That is a requirement of a life that facilitates the ministry of God, through your life and through mine. One of my favourite Greek words is the word for 'endurance'. It comes from two Greek words that were put together: *hupo-meno*. *Hupo* means 'under', *meno* means 'to remain'. What a graphic picture of endurance, that we remain under the pressure, we remain under the stress.

My mind races to Hebrews chapter 12, where this *hupo-meno* word is used again, in a very important context. At the end of chapter 11, people were stoned and sawn asunder, lived in caves and wore goat hair and were tortured. Then he brings us into chapter 12 and says, 'Now it is your turn to run the race and you are encompassed about with this great cloud of witnesses'. All these people from chapter 11 are around us, looking at our lives, saying, 'Take it forward. Finish what we've started. Endure like we endured. Stay under the pressure to get the job done!'

God hands us the baton of the race and we enter into that arena – it is an athletic metaphor – and we notice that our race is not on a smooth track. It is full of hurdles and obstacles, pain, suffering, seductions and disappointments. Paul, writing in Hebrews (I think he wrote Hebrews) says, 'Lay off those things that so easily beset you and run the race with endurance, with *hupo-meno*. Stay on track!' How do you do that? He goes on to say, 'looking unto Jesus, the author and finisher of our faith' (Heb. 12:2, NKJV). In every Roman arena there was an emperor's box. Emperor Jesus is sitting in the box with all these others of history surrounding him, watching us. It is our turn. We look to Jesus, the author and finisher of our faith and we run the race and endure, but there will be so many things that will want to distract us.

I remember when my oldest son, Joe, was about four. We decided he needed to learn how to swim. All the other kids were splashing, having a good time, and he takes one look at the water and starts bawling his eyes out. I had to take him back into the locker room. I said: 'You have got to do this.' He said, 'I don't want to learn how to swim. I am scared.'

I said, 'I will come to every lesson I possibly can. Every time you get scared, look up through the window and I will go like this, just to tell you it is going to be OK, hang in there, keep going.'

'Are you sure, Daddy?'

'Yeah, I am sure.'

'OK.' He went out and got started. He kept his eye on his father, not on the water, not on the fear. 'Looking unto Jesus, the author and finisher of our faith.' That is how we live to facilitate the treasure of the ministry of God through our lives of clay.

It is a strange thing that Paul would commend himself to the Corinthians with that kind of profile because the Corinthians were not into no-fault living. It was a wide open society, sensuality was everywhere. Getting some Puritan who has all these things he does not do – that does not go down well. And to be a servant? In a Corinthian society, it was the wealthy, the slick, the affluent, the ones that had the big houses, the ones that had the cool wardrobes, the ones that flaunted in the streets wearing purple – the sign of the aristocracy – they were the ones that counted. The servant didn't count. And to endorse suffering? Suffering people were out in Corinth! You did everything you could not to suffer. What a weird thing for him to say, 'This is what commends me to ministry.'

If that was all we had, it would be weird. But here is what makes it wonderfully not weird. Living in a no-fault zone as a servant who endures regardless is exactly the profile of Jesus Christ. We live as no-fault people, serving and enduring regardless, because we have a Saviour who lived a no-fault life, came to serve us, and endured regardless. This is the Jesus way. That is why we do this, that is why it commends us to effective life in ministry. I think about no-fault Jesus. I think about him before Pilate. Pilate interviews him behind closed doors and then he comes out before the people, who are clamouring for the blood of Christ. He washes his hands and says: 'I find no fault in him.'

In my life, I find it easy to find fault; with myself, with my friends, with my kids, sometimes with people I work with, with a lot of people who drive on the same streets I drive. I find it easy to find fault with people. I am so glad I have a Jesus that, after sixty years of following him, I have never seen a fault in him.

In America we have no-fault insurance for your cars. That means, if you get into an accident, they do not have to figure out who catches the blame, the insurance companies work it out. I am not for divorce but we have no-fault divorce, so if you want an express divorce, you do not have to blame anybody. It is a quick and easy thing. It does not begin to compare to having a no-fault Jesus who has served us. When the disciples are arguing in the upper room about who will be the greatest, Jesus rises, disrobes himself, takes his towel, puts it around his waist and does the most menial task of a servant. He draws a basin of water – the lowest of the house servants would have done this. He could not have gone lower to illustrate that God's followers serve. He washed their feet.

Taking up the cross

In Philippians chapter 2, we read that after Jesus accepted the form of a servant, he humbled himself and became obedient unto death, even the death of the cross. Back to Hebrews 12:2, we read, 'Looking unto Jesus, the author and finisher of our faith,' – who *hupo-menoed* – 'who endured the cross for the joy that was set before him.' As you walk in to the arena of your life and look at him, he lifts his nailed-scarred hand to you and says, 'You can do it. You can make it. Endure.' Because he is my no-fault, serving, enduring Saviour and he facilitated a ministry that has graced my life and our lives beyond comparison, I can say, 'I too, like him, will be living for that no-fault serving enduring life, that I might be like him.' I wonder if this is what he meant when he said, 'Take up your cross and follow me.' Could it be that he was talking about his kind of life, and that he asks us to live it as well?

What are we aiming for?

By Jeremy McQuoid

Jeremy McQuoid

Jeremy McQuoid is Teaching Pastor at Deeside Christian Fellowship, a growing independent evangelical church in the suburbs of Aberdeen. In addition to his weekly preaching and teaching ministry at Deeside, he speaks at conferences, and is particularly interested in training young men in preaching and church leadership. He and his wife, Elizabeth, have two sons.

What are we aiming for?
1 John 2:28 – 3:10

I do not know if you have heard the name Florence Chadwick. She was a long distance swimmer, and she became famous in August 1950 for being only the second woman to cross the English channel. But what most intrigued me about her story was a later attempt she made to swim a 21 mile stretch in California, called the Catalina Channel. After fifteen hours and 55 minutes of swimming, with only half a mile to go to the shore, and surrounded by boats full of friends and family who were cheering her on, Florence Chadwick gave up and asked to be taken out of the water.

When she was interviewed a little bit later on, no one could quite believe it. She was a champion swimmer, she was known for her endurance, so why had she stopped so close to the finish line? She said, 'It was the fog. If I could only have seen the shore, I know I would have made it.' But because she could not see the finish line, she felt like she was getting nowhere. With aching arms and aching limbs, she decided to give up.

Brothers and sisters, it is so important for us to know what we are aiming for in life, and to keep our eyes focused on it. In this passage tonight from 1 John, the writer tells us that there are two things especially we need to keep our eyes on as Christians. There are two fixed points that every Christian needs to keep in their sights, if we are going to live for Jesus in this dark world, and these two points are the two appearings of Jesus Christ. These two appearings of Jesus Christ should inspire us today to live holy and godly lives in this dark generation.

The word 'appearing' is the key word in this passage. It occurs six times, always with reference to Jesus Christ. John wants us, as believers, to live in the light of Christ's two appearings – his first appearing when he came to the cross to put away sin; and his second appearing, on that glorious future day when he will come in power and glory. True children of God, says John, live in light of these two great appearings.

Christ's second appearing

Notice that John puts the second appearing first in this passage. He begins by saying we need to live each day in the light of Christ's second appearing, his second coming (v. 28): 'And now, dear children, continue in him, so that when he appears we may be confident and unashamed before him at his coming.'

The word John uses here to describe Christ's second coming is the word *parousia*. This was the word that was used for a stunning formal occasion, when a king or an emperor would appear in all his royal regalia to celebrate a military triumph, and the streets would literally be lined, left to right, with people cheering. It was a ticker-tape reception, the crowds would be roaring. That is a reminder to us as believers that when Jesus Christ comes back to this world, it will be the most spectacular event that this Universe has ever seen. Jesus will not be coming back as the helpless little baby of Bethlehem; he will not be coming back as the frail man of sorrows hanging from a cross. He will return with eye-catching splendour. And the veil of his glorious person will be ripped away forever. His *parousia* will be the revelation, the apocalypse of the king of Glory, as he comes to claim this world as his own.

More than that, the second coming of Jesus Christ will not just be the unveiling of the Son of God: it will be the unveiling of the sons of God. Chapter 3 verses 1–2

How great is the love the Father has lavished on us, that we should be called children of God! And that is what we are! The reason the world does not know us is that it did not know him. Dear friends, now we are the children of God, and what we shall be has not yet been made known. But we know that when he appears, we shall be like him, for we shall see him as he is.

Our lives every day in this world are moving inexorably towards that glorious moment when Jesus Christ will burst through the clouds, and we will be changed in an instant, in the twinkling of an eye, at the last trumpet. As it says in 1 Corinthians 15, we shall be gloriously transformed from these weak, decaying, shameful earthly bodies, and we will be clothed in immortality. We will be indestructible: glorious and imperishable with heavenly bodies, that will look just like Christ's glorious resurrection body. When we see him, we shall be like him.

Brothers and sisters, we need to live each day with our eyes focused on the second coming of Christ. We will not only look like Jesus outwardly, we will look like him inwardly: we will be as pure and blameless as the Son of God himself. Can you take it in? That is our unshakeable destiny, as the sons and daughters of God. When we see him, we shall be like him. You were made to walk with Jesus in glory. This is God's plan for you from eternity to eternity. To be clothed in robes of light, to be transformed from the image of Adam, your fallen forefather, to the image of Jesus Christ, the perfect Son of God, the pioneer of a new humanity. This is your destiny. We live each day in the light of this glorious, triumphant moment, when the heavens open and we are caught up, as 1 Thessalonians says, to meet the Lord in the air. So we shall ever be with the Lord. Hallelujah. Praise the Lord – if we do not get excited about these things, there is something wrong with us.

Preparing for the second coming

John is not giving us this glorious vision of the second coming so that we can become star gazers, lost in wistful dreaminess. John wants to inspire us to godly living, here and now. If we go back to chapter 2:28, he says, 'Dear children, continue in him, so that when he appears we may be confident and unashamed.'

The challenge for every child of God is not to wait for this second coming. God is not asking us to wait for it. Waiting is a passive stance. Waiting develops a holy huddle mentality in the church, like people clasped together in underground bunkers during World War Two, while the bombs were dropping. John is not calling us to wait for the *parousia* of Christ. He is calling us to get ready for it. You have got to feel the urgency of John's words here. When Christ appears in awesome splendour, we will appear with him in glory and, John says, we want to be 'confident and unashamed' on that great day.

This implies, does it not, that I could be a blood bought child of God, and yet end up standing in front of Christ's throne on that great day – nervous, uncertain, even ashamed? Not because I am not a real believer, or because I have lost my salvation, that is impossible, but perhaps because I have squandered my days on earth. I am barely recognisable as a son of God. We have got to hear the challenge of John's words. Verse 29: 'If you know that he is righteous, you know that everyone who does what is right has been born of him.' The Jesus we are going to meet in the clouds on the last day is righteous. If we are claiming to be God's children, being transformed into the likeness of his Son with ever-increasing glory, then we have got to stand out from others in this world, who are not born again children of God.

John shows us here this tension that we live in every day. We are the dearly loved children of God. 'How great is the love the Father has lavished upon us' (1 John 3:1). The word is literally love from another world that God has shown us. How great is his love? But the world does not understand that. We live in a world that does not recognise us. Verse 2: 'The reason the world does not know us is that it did not know Christ.' We need to live righteous lives that reflect Jesus Christ in a world that neither recognises us, nor recognised him. Or, as Peter put it in his epistle, we need to live as 'aliens and strangers' in this world. That is the challenge. To live as children of God, in this world that does not know God or have any time for him. In a hostile world, we need to live each day in light of Christ's glorious second coming, when our true status as God's children will be revealed.

I sometimes ask myself, will it be a total shock to my friends and colleagues, to the people who see me in my street, to discover on that day that I am a child of God? Are you waiting for the second coming, as if you were in that underground bunker, or are you getting ready for it by living a transformed, provocative, attractive Christian life in this fading world? John commands us, as we look forward to Christ's second coming, to 'abide in Christ.' Abiding in Christ shows we are truly children who belong to another world.

What does abiding in Christ look like?

Are you, as John Stott used to put it, practising the presence of God in your life every day? Are you breathing in the air of eternity? Are you deliberately starting each day in God's presence? And I am talking here, quite deliberately, about the much maligned daily quiet time. This is how you live in the light of Christ's second coming.

In his book *The Crisis of Piety*, Donald Bloesch said, 'There is a crying need for the recovery of the devotional life . . . if anything characterises modern Protestantism, it is the absence of spiritual exercises. Yet such disciplines are the core of the life of devotion.' Those are two bad words in our generation: *exercises* – in a spiritual sense, and *disciplines*. And that quote by Donald Bloesch was from a chapter on journalling. What has struck me as I have read the biographies of some of the giants of the Christian faith – George Whitefield, John Wesley, Jim Elliot, great Puritans from the past like John Owen, women like Amy Carmichael – these men and women had deep devotional lives. The righteousness that characterises true children of God is impossible without disciplined devotional lives. These men and women were in the habit of journalling; of reading the Scriptures almost insatiably, and writing down what God was teaching them, putting it into their own words, until they owned it, and then mulling over the word of God.

These men and women were also powerfully active, but their activity for God was fuelled by this deep devotional life. They walked through this dying world breathing the air of eternity. Psalm 1 says, does it not, 'Blessed is the man who meditates on the law of the Lord day and night.' It is a 'through the day' thing. This Hebrew word for 'meditate' in Psalm 1 literally means 'to mutter'. Have you seen the Jews at the Wailing Wall, swaying back and forth, muttering to themselves? They are reciting passages of the Torah in the Old Testament. They have memorised Scripture and they are muttering it to themselves. That is the kind of vision Psalm 1 wants to give us, of a devotional life that we live in the word of God. We take it with us, we mutter it to ourselves throughout the day. Have we lost that daily quiet time, from which our whole lives spring?

Robert Murray McCheyne, that great Scottish pastor, gave out a daily reading plan to his congregation, which required them to read through the entire Old Testament once, and the New Testament and the Psalms twice every year. That was a requirement for every member of his congregation and they did that reading during the time of day when we watch *Eastenders* or search Amazon or update our contact list on our iPhone. We cannot complain of having a lack of time. It is how we prioritise our time. John Piper said the amount of time people spend on Facebook and Twitter shows we will have no excuse when Jesus condemns us on the last day for our prayerlessness.

Are you preparing for the second coming of Christ, by having this active, thirsty, disciplined daily quiet time? You are a child of God, you are going to stand with him one day in glory. Are you living like a child of God now, in preparation for your destiny? Do you stand out in your daily lifestyle, as a child of God, from your neighbours and colleagues? Is there something different about you? Is the way you use your money different? Have you lost out on a higher standard of living because you give so much of your income to church and mission activities? Do you drive a modest car and live simply, because you are a child of God who does not own anything in this world, who is looking forward to the next, sending all your baggage on ahead of you? Remember the Lausanne covenant that John Stott and Billy Graham signed, calling Christians in the West to live simply in an age of hunger, getting ready for the next life where our true riches are?

Are you getting your children ready for Jesus' return or are you getting them ready for life in this world? There is all the difference in the world. Do you want your children to be spiritual high flyers or just high flyers? Don Carson says he mourns over parents who are just beaming when their Jonny or Sally passes the bar exam or has just become a doctor, but show very little sadness when their children are going nowhere with Jesus. I would rather my children were hungry, poor, struggling with ill health and could not find a marriage partner but loved Jesus with all their hearts, than that they had it all but did not have him. 'For what shall it profit a man if he gains the whole world and loses his own soul?' John says, in verse 3, 'Everyone who has this hope in him purifies himself, just as he is pure.' John does not want us to wait for the second coming, but to get ready for it urgently.

Living in the light of the first coming

The true children of God live in the light of the two great appearings of Jesus Christ. We live, firstly, in the light of the second coming of Christ. But, John tells us in this passage, we also live in light of the first coming of Christ. That is a surprising angle he takes in verses 4 to 10 of chapter 3. He mentions Christ's first coming twice in these verses. In verse 5 John says, 'you know that he appeared [past tense] so that he might take away our sins.' Then again in verse 8, 'The reason the Son of God appeared was to destroy the devil's work.' So we look forward to the *parousia* of Christ, but we also look back to the cross of Christ, the reason Christ came in the first place. We need to live in the light of his first coming everyday, as well as his second coming. And the reason Christ came into our world in the first place was to rescue us from sin.

The atonement

This cardinal doctrine is being questioned today by many who call themselves evangelical. If there is one thing in Scripture we need to be crystal clear on, it is this issue. It is true that Christ died to demonstrate the love of God to us. It is true that he died to show us how we should love one another, to teach us to lay down our lives for each other. But if we leave it there, we are missing the bull's-eye of the gospel. Jesus Christ died to rescue us from sin. Christ died to take the punishment we deserve for our rebellion against a holy God. Christ died to absorb the righteous wrath of God against human sin, in his body on the tree. Christ died to take my hell for me. And I am hearing that 'h' word used less and less from pulpits. I hate the 'h' word but I have to use it as a gospel preacher, because God uses it again and again. He came to save me from hell. Or as John puts it in verse 5 here: Christ died 'so that he might take away our sins.' The cross of Christ is a picture of the horror of my sin and the length that a holy God had to go to deal with it.

John is telling us this, not just so that we will get our doctrine of the atonement right, however vital that is, but so that we will learn to hate sin in our own lives every day. We will learn to be as intolerant of sin in our own hearts as Jesus is. That is the point here. True children of God need to live in the light of Christ's first coming and Christ came to do away with sin. John is unsettled here by how easily Christians learn to live with the sin that nailed his Saviour to a cross. It is a complete contradiction, in John's mind, to call yourself a child of God, yet have a lax view of sin. Verse 4: 'Everyone who sins breaks the law; in fact, sin is lawlessness.' Verse 5: 'in him is no sin.' Verse 6: 'No one who lives in him keeps on sinning. No one who continues to sin has either seen him or known him.'

The moment that a believer trusts in Jesus Christ, he is declaring war for the rest of his days on the sin that nailed his Saviour to a cross. If sin is outright lawlessness, rebellion against the God we claim to love, and if Christ himself is the sinless one, then to go on sinning with impunity, with carelessness, after we have found Christ, is a complete contradiction. Christ came to destroy sin.

Can we be sinless?

We must be very careful here how we understand John's extreme language. John is always dealing in extremes. He loves to contrast light and darkness, death and life. He says, 'No one who lives in him keeps on sinning.' Is John teaching us here that a Christian can be sinless in this life? He cannot possibly be saying that because, back in chapter 1 he said if anyone claims to be without sin, he is a liar. That was the problem John had with the Gnostic false teachers: they were claiming sinlessness and he says 'Rubbish.' He calls on believers to confess our sins regularly to our forgiving God, who has dealt with our sins through the wrath-absorbing triumph of Christ on the cross. John is not teaching Wesleyan perfectionism here. We will never reach a point in this life when we are free from the influence of sin. But John is saying that as a Christian matures, he will – he must – become more and more intolerant of sin in his life.

I remember listening to Rico Tice speak about his weekly one to one sessions with John Stott at All Souls Church. Can you imagine having a one to one session every week with John Stott? During these sessions, John Stott would sometimes mention sin issues that he was struggling with, in his own life. Rico was often deeply challenged about this because, at times, John Stott would confess a sin that seemed so minor to Rico, it was hardly worth mentioning. It barely qualified as a sin. Yet this great man of God became deeply emotional about this seemingly irrelevant sin. He would be in tears sometimes, wondering how he could have failed his Lord so grievously. The closer a man gets to Christ, the more conscious he is of every shade of sin in his heart. And his goal in life is to crucify the flesh so that he can be a pure vessel ready to serve his holy Master. As Christians, we need to live in the light of Christ's first coming, and Christ came to put away sin.

When we spend time with the Lord, we learn to allow his word to search every corner of our beings, and all the while that word, through the Spirit, is unveiling to us in rich tapestries the holiness of God himself. The sinless Christ becomes more and more wonderful in my imagination. The closer I get to him, the more I see the full horror of my own sin: my pride, my selfishness, my desire for my own glory at God's expense; my gossip, my jealousy, my greed, the apathy that hangs around my soul like the mist hanging around the Keswick mountains. It is a painful process to go through, as the Holy Spirit places his scalpel on our souls but it is a good thing to go through, because it is a sign we are getting closer to the Holy One. The closer I get to Christ's magnificence, the more I feel my own wretchedness (Rom. 7:24). 'What a wretched man I am!' Like Isaiah in the temple, 'Holy, holy, holy is the Lord God of hosts. The whole earth is filled with his glory.' It pulsates with his glory. The reason why I have such a lax view of my own sin is because I have never really grasped how holy Jesus Christ is. There is no sin in him.

The High Priest in the Old Testament went into the Holy of Holies only once a year. He had to go through elaborate washing ceremonies just to prepare himself, and he could only enter through that seven inch thick curtain that separated the holy place of the Tabernacle from the Holy of Holies – once a year – if and only if he was carrying the blood of a sacrifice. Only if a little lamb had been taken and had his throat slit, only then, if he had followed all the procedures exactly, could he enter through that curtain. If, at that point, he did not have full reverence and fear for the God into whose presence he was trembling, he might die. That is exactly what happened to Aaron's sons in Leviticus 10. They offered unholy fire. We are not quite sure what that was, but they were consumed.

Have we distanced ourselves from those awesome Old Testament narratives? They're talking about Jesus. Have we forgotten how holy Jesus is? The closer you get to the flame, the more time you spend within the veil, the more the horror of your own sin glares at you in the radiance of his glory. 'Woe is me,' cries Isaiah, the most righteous man of his generation. 'Woe is me. I am ruined. My lips are unclean and I live among a people whose lips are unclean. My eyes have seen the king, the king of glory.'

The Christian who is spending time within the veil must grow more and more intolerant of every shadow of sin in his heart. That is why John uses extreme language to get to us. 'No one who continues to sin' – we might add the word 'wantonly' – 'has either seen Jesus or really got to know him at all'. We need to live every day in the light of Christ's first appearing and Jesus Christ came to destroy, came to obliterate, came to kick into touch, sin.

If you read about the great revivals in the history of the UK – 1904 in Cardiff, 1921 in East Anglia, stretching up to fishing villages in

Aberdeen, 1948 in the Hebrides – you knew that revival was coming when people became unusually aware of their sin, in the face of a holy God. That was the seedbed of revival. Chapels were open at 3 o'clock in the morning with people on their knees pleading for mercy.

I was reading about a young man in the Hebrides, who begged Duncan Campbell, the great revival preacher, not to come to his village because he so felt the weight of his sin. He could not bear the thought of a Spirit-filled evangelist exposing his soul to the glories of a holy God. And, if we are ever going to see revival again in our nation, this is where it starts, dare I say it, not with holy laughter but with holy tears. Children of God, live in the light of Christ's first coming. Christ came to destroy sin, so how can we play with, how can we tolerate, the thing he despises?

When we sin, says John, we actually live like children of the devil. That is how starkly John puts it in verses 7 to 10 here. We get in bed with Satan every time we sin. Verse 8: 'He who does what is sinful is of the devil, because the devil has been sinning from the beginning.' Jesus said in John's Gospel, 'Sin is his mother tongue.' Verse 10: 'This is how we know who the children of God are, and who the children of the devil are.' Not if they have signed an evangelical statement of faith and come to the Keswick Convention, but if they absolutely hate sin in their hearts because they've fallen absolutely in love with Jesus. Every time we sin, we raise a toast to Satan, and we mock the cross of Christ. Do we feel that in our souls tonight? Or is there – and I am searching my own heart as much as yours – a certain kind of sin that we are learning to tolerate in our lives and in our churches?

It is interesting, if you read the seven letters to the churches in Revelation, how many times the word 'tolerate' is used. Sins like gossip, lust and rivalry are prevalent sins in middle class churches but they are rarely confronted. Yet they are satanic. Jesus called lust, adultery. He called gossip, murder, because it is murdering someone's character. We think of gossip as something we do to keep things exciting in church. When Jesus thinks of gossip, he feels spikes in his head.

Jesus was nailed to the cross for my gossip, my jealousies, my white lies, my broken promises and the favouritism I show in church to the people I prefer; my laziness, my apathy, my impatience, and my slandering of leaders in the church. Jesus was spat upon, bruised and brutalised, made to look like half a man, to pay the price for the things I tolerate, for the things I play around with, as I raise my glass to Satan, and trample on the cross of Jesus Christ. There is forgiveness and amazing grace to cover every stain but it is not cheap grace. If we really knew this grace, we would start to hate the sin that calls for this grace. True children of God cannot tolerate any shade of sin in their lives.

I wonder if the mist is clearing for you yet and you can see, in your mind now, the two great focal points that you need to keep your eyes on, as you try and live a godly life in Christ Jesus. You need to keep your eyes focused on the second coming of Christ, for one day you will be dressed in robes of white and you will stand at his side in glory. Don't wait for that, get ready for that. And you need to keep your heart focused on the first coming of Christ, when he died to obliterate sin or, as the Old Testament keeps on telling us: 'Be ye holy, even as I the Lord your God am holy.' And the people of God said, Amen.

Harvest time

by Peter Maiden

Peter Maiden

Peter Maiden is International Director of Operation Mobilisation and a Trustee of Keswick Ministries. He travels extensively to fulfil his commitments with OM, which has staff in 116 countries. Peter serves on the board of a number of other Christian groups, is an elder of Hebron Evangelical Church in Carlisle and an Honorary Canon of Carlisle Cathedral. Peter enjoys family life with his wife, Win, and their three grown-up children and eight grandchildren.

Harvest time: John 12:20–36

Introduction

As I travel around the world, in every nation I meet people who are on the mission field because they heard the call of God on a night like this at the Keswick Convention. It is amazing what God does, on nights like this. Two or three years ago, I was preaching on mission night and I made the appeal. I saw an elderly man, in his eighties, walking to the front. I knew he had been a missionary in India all of his life, so I wondered what on earth he was doing, making a response to this appeal. I went down to him at the end and said, 'Brother, what are you doing here?' He said, 'I feel God is calling me to move to an old people's home. He wants me to be his ambassador in that home, and that is why I am responding.'

It is harvest time

I want to speak to you tonight about the mission of Jesus. Not long ago, I was speaking at a church in South Korea. The first service was at 6.30 on the Sunday morning and four thousand people were in their seats. Further services followed at 8.30, 10.30, 12.30 – all completely full to overflowing, Four thousand people at each service. Just imagine that, in one church, four times every Sunday they have larger congregations than we have here this evening.

Horace Allen and Horace Underwood, who started their mission to Korea in 1884, finally saw their first convert two years later in 1886. They could never have dreamed of the ultimate results of what they had begun under God. For a period of time, churches in Korea, according to one survey, were seeing a growth in membership every year of between thirteen and fifteen percent. That was between six and seven hundred per cent higher than the national annual population growth which was about two per cent. So four thousand churches were being planted every year in South Korea; ten new churches every day.

Early next year, I will be speaking at the Maramon convention in India. We will be seeing crowds then not of thousands but of tens of thousands and, on the weekend, more than a hundred thousand, coming to hear the word of God. I am telling you this so that you recognise it is harvest time in the worldwide church. Sometimes we do not get that impression, living in Western Europe. I have been going to India for thirty years. We go once a year and gather all our OM leaders together from around the country, and we have prayer and reports. For the first twenty years, there would be reports of five Hindus being converted in the past year in this area, ten maybe in this area and it was big news when a new church was planted. Today, I hear not of the one or the tens but the scores, indeed the hundreds of churches, being planted amongst the Dalits every year.

A friend of mine was preaching in a Muslim country just a couple of years ago, where there is a real move of God going on amongst one people group. He was there for a couple of days teaching the Bible. It was a small room, packed full and very hot. Then, all of a sudden, as they continued worshipping, the crowd divided and went to the corners of the room. An elderly lady moved out of the crowd that was dispersing and began to sing and dance in the area that had been vacated. Howard said to his interpreter, 'Why is she doing what she is doing?' The interpreter said, 'She has been a Muslim all her life. She comes from one of the villages close to here and last Sunday she trusted the Lord Jesus Christ, in her eighty-second year.' This was the first time she had been able to worship with other Christians.

The statisticians tells us that in AD 100, for every 360 non-Christians, there was one Christian. By 1900, it was down to 27 non-Christians for every Christian. By the year 2000, it was 6.8 non-Christians for every Christian. Have you ever met .8 of a non-Christian? I am told they are a little easier to evangelise than a fully orbed non-Christian. I am not sure what this statistician's definition of 'Christian' is, but all of this shows it is harvest time in the world-wide church.

The climax of his mission

Where did it all begin? Jesus is in Jerusalem and it is Passover time. Some estimate that up to three million people would be in the city on such an occasion. Among them are some Greek visitors and they come to Philip with a very simple request. Translated into English, it is just seven words: 'Sir, we would like to see Jesus.' Then they disappear from the scene, never to be heard from again. But this request is an indication to Jesus that the climax of his mission has arrived. 'The hour has come,' is his response, 'for the Son of Man to be glorified.' This brief contact with these Greek visitors shows that the time has come for Jesus to die for the world. As Leon Morris puts it; 'He no longer belongs to Judaism, which in any case has rejected him. But the world, whose Saviour he is, awaits him and seeks for him.'

I wonder if, at that moment, Jesus saw the millions on the African continent, the millions in India, in Latin America and indeed all over the world today who are worshipping him. It is an amazing phenomenon. Samuel Escobar expresses it like this

> The word became flesh and lived for a while among us in Palestine during the first century of our era. After that the story has moved from culture to culture, nation to nation, people to people. And something strange and paradoxical has taken place. Though Jesus was a peasant from Palestine everywhere he has been received, loved and adored, and people in hundreds of cultures and languages have come to see the glory of God in the face of Jesus Christ. Moreover they have come to see that he is theirs.

He is not a British Jesus, he is not an American Jesus, he is 'theirs'. And we know that this will continue. Steve Brady has already quoted from Revelation. 'After this I looked and before me there was a great multitude that no one could count, from every nation' – just as God had promised to Abraham centuries before – 'from every nation, tribe, people and language, standing before the throne and in front of the lamb. They were wearing white robes and were holding palm trees in their hands. And they cried out in a loud voice. "Salvation belongs to our God, who sits on the throne and to the lamb."'

Jesus is the Saviour of the whole world. Do we believe that? Paul certainly did. Remember how he instructs Timothy to train the churches he is establishing to pray. As he trains them to pray, he urges them that 'prayers, intercession and thanksgiving be made for everyone – for kings and all those in authority, that we may live peaceful and quiet lives in all godliness and holiness.' But then Paul continues: 'This is good and pleases God our Saviour who wants all men to be saved and to come to a knowledge of the truth.'

God is the Saviour and he wants all people to be saved. That means not just Jews but Gentiles, not just the rich but the poor – and not just the poor, but the rich. Paul bases his case on two realities. First of all, he says, 'For there is only one God.' In the Old Testament this statement was used to counteract the polytheistic claims of the pagan religions. But here Paul is going a massive step further. He is arguing that the oneness of God means that all peoples must have access to the salvation of this one God. He makes the same point in Romans 3:29–30: 'After all God is not the God of the Jews only, is he? Isn't he also the God of the Gentiles?' Of course he is. There is only one God, and there is only one way of being accepted by him. He makes people right with himself only by faith, whether they are Jews or Gentiles.

Could we not ask exactly the same question? He is not the God of the British only, is he? He is not only the God of the Western world or even only the God of the Global South. He is not the God only of the evangelised areas of our world. Isn't this one God the God of the Tibetans, the Tajiks, the Turkmens, the Kashmiris? He is the God of the deprived areas of our nation, where even our police can only go in groups for safety. He is not just the God of the leafy suburbs. Somehow the gospel must penetrate everywhere, for there is only one God.

In the world of missions we often refer to 'people groups', ethnic groups who have their own sense of identity. Mission researchers have sought to discover how many people groups there are in the world, and there are different ways of calculating this. The most reliable, probably, comes up with 16,536 different ethnic people groups in the world. The estimate is that today 6,829 of them remain unreached, meaning there is no indigenous community of believing Christians with the resources to evangelise their own people. Two thousand years after Jesus issued his command to disciple the nations, with all the resources we have at our fingertips today, over 40 per cent of the world's people groups are still saying, 'Come, tell us of this one God who has provided salvation for all peoples.'

The universal access to this one God, says Paul, which the work of mission must provide, is only through one mediator. 'There is one God,' writes Paul, 'and one mediator between God and men, the man Christ Jesus who gave himself as a ransom for all.' In John 12:32, Jesus says: 'But I, when I am lifted up from the earth, will draw all men to myself.' The 'I' there is emphatic. This is a work for Christ and no one else. He is the *only* mediator.

The request of these Greek visitors indicates to Jesus that the climax of his mission has arrived. He is to be the Saviour for all. Their request was to see Jesus, and Jesus seems to be saying 'Yes! You will certainly see me, and tens of millions, indeed hundreds of millions, throughout the world will see me.' The climax of his mission has arrived.

The clarity of his mission

What's on the mind of Jesus as this climatic moment arrives? What's his motivation? It is very clear, verse 28: 'Father glorify your name.' That cry comes in a time of huge emotional and spiritual struggle. But it is, as Bruce Milne puts, 'the ultimate passion of his being.' 'Father, I want to see your name glorified.' Why do we do what we do? Why do we organise this Convention? Why do I prepare and preach a message like this? Why have so many, over the centuries, been ready to sacrifice their lives? Why are as many as one out of every ten Christians willing to suffer persecution today? Why? Because we want to see the name, the character, of God our Father glorified. That was at the heart of the mission of Jesus Christ and it must be at the heart of our mission as the people of God. John Piper famously said, 'Mission exists where worship does not.' That is why we send people to the unreached peoples, of both our world and our streets. God is not being worshipped there, and he demands and alone deserves to be worshipped. So, as Jesus reaches the climax of his ministry, to become the Saviour of the world, his focus is absolutely clear: 'Father I want to see your name glorified.' And then Jesus explains the heart of his mission.

The centre of his mission

Verse 24 says: 'I tell you the truth, unless a kernel of wheat falls to the ground and dies, it remains only a single seed. But if it dies, it produces many seeds.' There is no salvation without the death of Christ; no gospel to proclaim without Calvary; no mission which does not have, at its centre, the proclamation of the substitutionary death of the Lord Jesus.

At this time, more than any other, Jesus was the man of the moment. That is why the Greeks were seeking him. That is why the Pharisees, in prophetic frustration, said in verse 19: 'The whole world has gone after him.' Look at verse 12: 'the great crowd that had come for the Feast heard that Jesus was on his way to Jerusalem. They took palm branches and went out to meet him, shouting,

"Hosanna!" . . . "Blessed is the King of Israel!"' He is the man of the moment. Verse 18 says: 'Many people, because they had heard that he had given this miraculous sign [that is the raising of Lazarus] went out to meet him.'

It almost seems as if Jesus has got the world at his feet. He seems to be enjoying an earthly triumph, and surely he will go on from here to even greater things. He will use his popularity and his obvious powers to deliver Israel. But no: 'unless a kernel of wheat falls to the ground and dies, it remains only a single seed. But if it dies, it produces many seeds.' The great divine principle is that life comes through death. Eternal life for the many will come through the death of the one. 'God kills' writes Tasker 'to make alive.' It is a paradox but a vital one to understand. We'll never understand the Christian life, we'll certainly never understand the work of Christian mission, without embracing this principle – 'The way to fruitfulness lies through death.'

The consequences of his mission

The Father will be glorified

We have seen that was the heart cry of Jesus, the motive behind all that he did. The strength of this motivation overcame everything else. The prospect of the crucifixion, taking upon himself the whole burden of human sin: the horror, the shame of evil, throws the soul of Jesus into temporary turmoil. The language used here is extremely strong and it implies utter revulsion at the prospect. Verse 27: 'Now my heart is troubled, and what shall I say? "Father, save me from this hour"?' Interpreters are divided here, differing over whether this was the actual prayer of our Saviour, or a hypothetical prayer, a question: 'Am I to say, "Father, save me from this hour?"' Whichever way it should be understood, immediately Jesus again recognises the divine will and purpose that has brought him to this hour. We have seen the clarity of his focus: 'Father, glorify your name.'

The response in heaven to this cry is heard on earth (vs. 28–29): '"I have glorified it, and will glorify it again." The crowd that was there and heard it said it had thundered; others said an angel had spoken to him.' The desire of Jesus was that, through his sacrifice, the truth about his Father would be recognised. The love, the mercy, the righteousness, the justice of his Father – they would be demonstrated and clearly seen at the cross. The assurance of the Father as Jesus goes forward to Calvary is that that will be done.

Many seeds will be produced (v. 24)

Jesus was absolutely clear that his death and, as we have seen, only his death, would open the door of heaven to all believers. Those at that moment scattered throughout Gentile heathen lands would be brought in to the new Israel, the people of God, and they would come from every tribe, tongue and nation.

I mentioned earlier the staggering growth of the church in recent days. Imagine that this congregation in Keswick this evening was representative of the Christian church worldwide. At least two-thirds of this congregation would be non-Western and there would be many more black and coloured faces than white faces. The death of the one has led to the life of the many, and this growth will go on and on and on until the church is complete, the Bride is ready and the Bridegroom returns.

Judgement on this world (v. 30)

The crucifixion of the Son of Man exposes the sin of the human race. The facts are undeniable. God, in his love, sent his Son into the world, and the world utterly rejected and slew him. Sin has been exposed in its most dreadful, most ugly form, at the cross. But, and this is truly amazing, Jesus in his death not only exposes our guilt and shame, but he becomes the guilty one. As our substitute, our sacrificial lamb, he bears our judgement for us. What a message, what a gospel, what good news we have, through the cross! Guilt and shame can be dealt with, however dreadful that guilt and shame might be. The very one who exposes our guilt and shame at the cross takes that guilt and shame upon himself.

The prince of this world driven out (v. 30)

As Jesus hung on the cross, it must have appeared to be a complete victory for Satan. A watching world could not see that this was his moment of utter defeat. Jesus carries his perfect obedience as a man to the will of God to its terrible conclusion. In doing so, he breaks forever the chains of guilt, shame and condemnation that had bound us. From that moment, what John saw by revelation was inevitable:

'The kingdom of the world has become the kingdom of our Lord and of his Christ' (Rev. 11:15). It is true, of course, as John writes in his first epistle 'to this hour the world is under the control of the evil one.' But the kingdom is established, the power is broken: as Luther wrote – 'His doom is writ.' And we will finally see what John saw in Revelation, Satan 'hurled down' (Rev. 12:10).

Jesus himself will be glorified (v. 23)

Jesus will be lifted up: physically lifted up at the cross but also glorified. Imagine the reaction when Jesus said the hour had come for him to be glorified. As Barclay puts it; 'The listeners would catch their breath, they would believe that the trumpet call of eternity had sounded, the might of heaven was on the march. But Jesus did not mean by glorified what they meant. He meant crucified.' As Milne puts it; 'The cross is a throne, his crucifixion is his coronation. He is not glorified as a reward or recompense for the cross. His death is his exaltation. We must not see the cross as defeat and the resurrection as victory. Jesus won the victory at the cross and the resurrection demonstrates and proclaims that victory.'

The outstretched arms of Jesus say the doors are now open to all men and women, every tribe, every tongue, every nation, every street in every city of this nation. Your king says come, the barriers are down, the power of the enemy is broken. That is the mission of Jesus. It has reached its climax. He will be the Saviour of the world.

What does this mean for us?

A message for the whole world

We must have people in every nation, every people group, and also in every aspect of society in this nation, shining as lights. No one is to be excluded. Our gospel is exclusive, in the sense that it is only through Christ being uplifted that people can be drawn by God to salvation, but it is *inclusive* in its reach. It is for all who will believe. God may be calling some in this meeting this evening to new steps of obedience, in order to ensure that this message of one God and one mediator goes to all peoples. It is a tragedy that two thousand years after Jesus issued his command, more than 40 per cent of the world's peoples are still saying, 'Come.' It is a tragedy that there are people in our cities, in our villages, in this country, who still do not clearly understand the message of salvation. We have a message for all.

Our focus must mirror our Saviour's

We minister for the glory of God alone. The work we are involved in will often be disappointing, and sometimes people will disappoint us. If we work for our own satisfaction or to be appreciated and applauded by others, then I fear for us. This is the only motive that will carry us through rough times: 'God, this is not about me, my popularity, my comfort, even my survival. It is about you. It is about your glory.' This is such a tricky issue for fallen human beings. OM is quite a big mission, the largest mission in certain aspects of missionary endeavour around the world, and sometimes OM people come to me and say, 'Peter, we are now the largest . . .' I stop them. I say, 'What point are you trying to make? This is not about us, it is not about size, it is not about popularity. It is about God and his glory. It is about people seeing his majesty, amongst the nations and evident on the streets of our cities. It is for the whole world and the focus must be his glory.'

Life comes through death

The grain of wheat must die if life is to be seen. What was true for the Lord Jesus as he approached the cross is also true for us. Jesus made that very clear. After speaking of the necessity for his own death in verse 24, he continues in verse 25: 'The man who loves his life will lose it, while the man who hates his life in this world will keep it for eternal life. Whoever serves me must follow me; and where I am, my servant also will be. My Father will honour the one who serves me.' I find it deeply moving, in John 12, as we see the enormous struggle Jesus has to go through if his mission is to be accomplished and the will of his Father is to be done. I ask myself, 'Am I to expect that the mission God has called me to will be without struggle, without self - sacrifice?'

We know that Satan is implacably opposed to this mission being accomplished even though he knows his 'doom is writ.' So the opposition will continue and indeed increase, right to the end. A price will continually have to be paid. God may have been calling you for some time. You know a new step of faith is called for, which may take you to an unreached people group or to another part of your city. It may be the realisation that you are Christ's ambassador in your place of work or your neighbourhood and, from tonight onwards, your approach is going to be entirely different. I will never forget an old man, walking to the front, called by God to be an ambassador in an old people's home. Think of the hundreds of missionaries all around the world, serving God right now amongst the peoples of the world, trace their call right back to this tent and a night such as this.

Keswick 2010

Keswick Convention 2010 teaching is available now
All Bible readings and talks recorded at Keswick 2010, including
Don Carson, Steve Brady, Paul Mallard, Joe Stowell, Liam Goligher
and Jonathan Lamb are available now on CD, MP3 download and
DVD★ from www.essentialchristian.com/keswick

Keswick teaching now available on MP3 download
Just select the MP3 option on the teaching you want, and after
paying at the checkout your computer will receive the teaching
MP3 download – now you can listen to teaching on the go;
on your iPod, MP3 player or even your mobile phone.

Over fifty years of Keswick teaching all in one place
Visit www.essentialchristian.com/keswick to browse Keswick
Convention Bible teaching as far back as 1957! You can also browse
albums by worship leaders and artistes who performed at Keswick,
including Stuart Townend, Phatfish and Keith & Kristyn Getty, plus
Keswick Live albums and the *Precious Moments* collection of DVDs.

To order, visit www.essentialchristian.com/keswick or call 0845
607 1672

★Not all talks available on DVD.

KESWICK MINISTRIES

Keswick Ministries is committed to the deepening of the spiritual life in individuals and church communities through the careful exposition and application of Scripture, seeking to encourage the following:

Lordship of Christ – To encourage submission to the Lordship of Christ in personal and corporate living
Life Transformation – To encourage a dependency upon the indwelling and fullness of the Holy Spirit for life transformation and effective living
Evangelism and Mission – To provoke a strong commitment to the breadth of evangelism and mission in the British Isles and worldwide
Discipleship – To stimulate the discipling and training of people of all ages in godliness, service and sacrificial living
Unity – To provide a practical demonstration of evangelical unity

Keswick Ministries is committed to achieving its aims by:

• providing Bible based training courses for youth workers & young people (via Root 66) and Bible Weeks for Christians of all backgrounds who want to develop their skills and learn more
• promoting the use of books, downloads, DVDs and CDs so that Keswick's teaching ministry is brought to a wider audience at home and abroad
• partnering with Christian TV and radio stations so that superb Bible talks can be broadcast to you at home
• publishing up-to-date details of Keswick's exciting news and events on our website so that you can access material and purchase Keswick products on-line
• publicising Bible teaching events in the UK and overseas so that Christians of all ages are encouraged to attend 'Keswick' meetings closer to home and grow in their faith
• putting the residential accommodation of the Convention Centre at the disposal of churches, youth groups, Christian organisations and many others, at very reasonable rates, for holidays and outdoor activities in a stunning location

If you'd like more details please look at our website (www.keswickministries.org) or contact the Keswick Ministries office by post, email or telephone as given below.

**Keswick Ministries, Convention Centre, Skiddaw Street,
Keswick, Cumbria, CA12 4BY
Tel: 017687 80075; Fax: 017687 75276;
email: info@keswickministries.org**

Keswick 2011

Week 1: 16th – 22nd July
Week 2: 23rd – 29th July
Week 3: 30th July – 5th August

The annual Keswick Convention takes place in the heart of the English Lake District, an area of outstanding national beauty. It offers an unparalled opportunity to listen to gifted Bible exposition, meet Christians from all over the world and enjoy the grandeur of God's creation. Each of the three weeks has a series of morning Bible readings, and then a varied programme of seminars, lectures, book cafes, prayer meetings, concerts, drama and other events throughout the day, with evening meetings that combine worship and teaching. There is also a full programme for children and young people, with week 1 seeing a return of Abide, meetings aimed specifically at those aged 19–24. Causeway Prospects will be running a series of meetings for those with learning difficulties in week 2. K2, the interactive track for those in their twenties and thirties, also takes place in week 2. There will be a special track for the deaf in week 3.

The theme for Keswick 2011 is *Word to the World: Good News to the Nation*
The Bible readings will be given by:
Ajith Fernando (week 1) on Jonah
Chris Wright (week 2) Bible Overview
Peter Maiden (week 3) on 2 Timothy

Other confirmed speakers are Bill Bygroves, Steve Brady, Ken Clarke, Patrick Fung, Liam Goligher, Krish Kandiah, Jonathan Lamb, Michael Nazir-Ali and Amy Orr-Ewing.★

★ Speakers' list correct at time of going to press. Check out the website for further details.